# Contents

## A Tribute to a Great Soldier

We had all heard of Clive of India from our history books, but the true hero of this century was undoubtedly Field Marshal Slim — Uncle Bill to his 14th Army troops. Through his skill as a professional soldier he personally instigated the masterstroke which put paid to the myth of Japanese invincibility in South-East Asia. Like him, we all suffered humiliation during the early years of the war in Burma, partly through gross tactical errors and limited resources, prior to Slim gaining ultimate command.

Some troops in the forward areas knew little of his influence until after the big push from late 1944 onwards, and even then it was many years after the war before the true calibre of this great general emerged.

As an extra, very ordinary part-time soldier, I salute his memory and remind those survivors still with us that we all owe to him, Uncle Bill, our very survival today — *We shall remember him.*

Bill Bryden
(gunner-signaller) RA (TA)
and the Royal Scots

# SHELL-SHOCKED!

## from
## ARAKAN to MANDALAY
## (1942-1945)

## Bill Bryden

**(gunner-signaller) (private) Royal Artillery**

**and Royal Scots, XIVth ARMY**

ARTHUR H. STOCKWELL LTD.
Torrs Park  Ilfracombe  Devon
*Established 1898*
*www.ahstockwell.co.uk*

*British Library Cataloguing-in-Publication Data.*
*A catalogue record for this book is available*
*from the British Library.*

*Arthur H. Stockwell Ltd., bear no responsibility*
*for the accuracy of events recorded in this book.*

*To fallen comrades and those still with us,*
*we shall remember them.*

ISBN 0 7223 3621-7
*Printed in Great Britain by*
*Arthur H. Stockwell Ltd.*
*Torrs Park   Ilfracombe*
*Devon*

# Foreword

Readers must realise the manner in which this factual story was compiled and written. As an ordinary ranker in the British Army, no front-line soldiers were allowed to carry diaries, or had access to any classified documents; in fact, army regulations stated that only a soldier's pay book and identity discs were allowed in forward areas. On the other hand, the writer was often in a position as a signaller to know what was happening around him and Intelligence at Brigade and Divisional HQ relied heavily on daily dispatches being sent back by wireless, field-telephone or dispatch riders. In short, the Signals personnel were a vital link in the LOC (lines of communications), reporting daily on ration strength (which referred to number of personnel in the unit that day), ammunition expenditure, petrol, etc., etc. We in return received coded weather reports in a series of five-figure groupings to assist in command post range conversions when preparing a shoot (or barrage), vital to the accuracy of the shells when in flight towards a distant enemy target. I must add that there were no press or army reporters in the earlier campaigns either. To many, what happened in late 1942 and early 1943 was a closed book, and this account might help to put the record straight even to self-motivated historians. In short, we were the umbilical cord on which our rear-echelon Intelligence staff slavishly depended, otherwise their records were incomplete. This system worked well until communications broke down, such as when forward units were surrounded or captured. Then only the men on the spot knew what was happening, that is why parts of this story could be misconstrued by intelligence sources far behind the field of battle.

This account was written not to glorify life in the British Army during World War Two, but as a factual experience which could reflect on the minds of those other ordinary blokes who were temporarily classified as 'Civilians in Uniform'.

The accounts related in this book would be better classified as a series of essays, grouped to form a somewhat haphazard record between 1939 and 1946, allowing for a certain amount of overlap. This method of approach is not orthodox in the mind of a professional novelist, but as events took place, life in the war was also haphazard. In the eyes of many of us, there was a recurring amount of confusion and uncertainty as we were subjected to food shortages over long periods and being treated as second-class citizens by our own hierarchy. Readers must realise that this story could only be conceived by a somewhat indelible memory and the human reflections were portrayed from the heart of a very sincere but humble person, perhaps like yourself.

Now read on . . .

*Bren Gun Carrier*

# Shell-Shocked!

*Kilmarnock — 1939:*
It was Friday, 1st September 1939, World War Two was all but declared. I was employed by Messrs Glenfield and Kennedy, hydraulic engineers, Kilmarnock. News came during the afternoon while at work: all Territorial and other Reserve personnel were told to report to their respective military depots throughout the British Isles. I got home just after five, washed and changed, had my dinner, then reported at the RA drill hall in John Finnie Street. We had only got back from camp three weeks before and had left our uniforms, etc. in our kitbags for storage. We signed for our gear while waiting for our medical check-up. I noticed how young looking we all were; a few of the lads were still only seventeen, I had turned eighteen in April and signed on one week later for four years as a 'fireside soldier'! Now there was a declared emergency and suddenly we became regulars for the duration of that emergency.

After everybody had been medically examined, we paraded inside the drill hall to hear an announcement thanking us for a prompt and almost 100% turnout — one or two stragglers were out of town and joined us later. One comment was made that although we were generally fit medically, most of us required building up physically, as the previous depression years had been lean on the diet of the up-and-coming generation.

Those who could, returned to their respective homes for the night. As we went outside, it was now dark and the usually brightly lit streets were gloomy and eerie. Buses moved by slowly, picking their way through the crowds thronging the streets, all headlamps were masked, others used parking lights only. Inside the buses, blue-coated light bulbs shone dimly above the centre passages only. We all sensed that sinking feeling that war was inevitable and an unpredictable gloom lurked in the foreboding darkness. Everyday schedules no longer existed. Almost at once it all began to happen; hand-held torches began to appear as lamp standards suddenly became a hazard in the blackout. There was no longer any light-hearted laughter, and a rekindling of patriotism began to emerge like an aura among the citizens of every community. We cast aside our individual ideals and closed ranks. It had all happened spontaneously during the course of one evening, only the formalities remained and Prime Minister Chamberlain made the formal declaration of war two days later on Sunday, 3rd September 1939 at 11 a.m. GMT.

On that Sunday morning, around 11.15 a.m., our battery, known as the 316th, was mustered across John Finnie Street. We were now in our battledress uniforms, wearing forage caps while the officers paraded with Sam Brownes, cheese cutters and canes. This was to be a show of preparedness to reassure the people of Kilmarnock that their sons were ready and willing to defend their freedom. We stood to attention at open order for inspection. My battery commander stood to my right front as I stood motionless in the front rank, staring straight ahead into a monumental mason's yard. People lined the pavements as orders were being barked by senior NCOs and warrant officers. Cold shivers ran up my spine as I stood among my new-found comrades. Suddenly, a motherly woman in a crowd of onlookers came towards me pointing at me and crying out with a distraught look in her lined face: "He's just a boy, look at him, not a day older than fifteen. It's a damned shame! It's no right, they should send him home!"

The lady had to be restrained and finally my battery commander broke ranks and came over to her saying, "It's all right, missus, the lad is eighteen. I should know for I'm his manager at the Glenfield!"

The lady withdrew still not fully convinced. I could never forget the atmosphere that day: grown men openly wept as we marched along King Street, hankies reflected the thoughts among the people of Kilmarnock — how could we ever forget them?

When not filling sandbags, we went on route marches and signallers practised the Morse code, etc. while the gunners were drilled on the World War One 4.5 howitzer guns. These were mounted on wooden-wheeled gun carriages. Ironically the guns had a stencilled sign on them which said 'US for drill purposes only'. Men on guard duty were 'armed' with a military cane as there were no rifles either. In short, we were unarmed and some men had to wear their own boots, possibly due to their size not being available at the QM stores. We had neither steel helmets nor respirators (army), so we carried our civilian gas masks in a cardboard box. Britain had the manpower but equipment was a long way off. The only uniform we had was the one we stood up in, it had to do for parades and all other duties. We slept in them on manoeuvres and guard duties, but always endeavoured to have them presentable with a crease in our trousers when off duty. There were no beds, sheets or mattresses, and we slept on floors head to tail in unventilated buildings. Windows, etc. had to be blacked out every night before dark and blackouts were left on as a fixture. The build-up of foul air was punctuated with cigarette smoke, body heat and foul-smelling,

8

dank humidity. It was a long winter! Somehow we survived but it said little for the 'planners' down in Whitehall. We all knew war was inevitable, but basic equipment and billets took a back seat in military strategy. Only the Boy Scouts had the motto 'Be Prepared'.

About a month later, the battery was ordered to assemble and proceed to an undisclosed destination (for security reasons). We embarked on a fleet of Western SMT coaches; the drivers did not know or disclose where we were going. The convoy headed east, which meant nothing to us. However, as all signposts had been removed, we could only guess. We saw names like Biggar and Peebles on shop signs, and it was not long before we arrived at a quaint, wee Border town called Selkirk, nestling among the wooded hills and streams far from the hustle and bustle of any industrial metropolis. Yet, for all the secrecy, as we stopped at the Victoria Halls along the High Street, there standing proudly by the front entrance was a handsomely painted sign notifying all passers-by that this was the headquarters of the 130th Field Regiment, Royal Artillery, and the gun insignia was neatly displayed in the centre.

The public had been well informed of our arrival and made us most welcome. The Borderers are well known for their hospitality and are hard to beat for their sincerity — it must be down to the quiet orderly way of life that they live as opposed to harsher environments experienced by others in other areas and the consequent coarser and more contemptuous attitudes emanating from different cultures.

We all slept in neat rows head to tail across the main floor of the Victoria Hall, while the bandsmen billeted themselves on the stage and the officers roughed it at the County Hotel! A field-kitchen cookhouse was put up along the Chapel Street side of the building, and we were told that there were public baths at the Institute along the High Street. As we were extremely overcrowded, some of us were later transferred along Chapel Street to the West Church Hall, others were put into the Volunteer Hall in the (under) Back Row (street). Our pipe band soon got organised and before long the troops were marching in church parades and routemarches to tunes like 'Rowan Tree', 'Bonnie Galloway', 'Geordie's Byre', 'The Somme Lament' and last but not least, 'Blue Bonnets O'er the Border'. The boys from Galloway linked up with us and they, the 315th Battery, were billeted in the Haining Estate at the other end of the town.

The Regiment was privileged to be entertained at the Victoria Hall by none other than Sir Harry Lauder and a very talented company in full Highland regalia. They had us singing and laughing in a way few could have found possible, and our mean-and-miserly image of Harry Lauder was scotched once and for all. His theme song that night was, 'Singing is the Thing to Make You Cheery', which became well known.

There were indiscernible figures shuffling past at intervals, some homeward bound, others going in the direction of the 'toon' as I stood on guard duty. The night was cold and draughty outside by the main gate at the entrance to the Victoria Hall. Occasionally a voice would croak, "Gie snell sentry!" as a figure moved on into the gloom. I was alerted when one shortened figure of a man stopped and grunted, "Gie cauld, whith fet the nicht?"

I agreed and reiterated, "Gie cauld but could be worse."

The voice then asked when I would be off duty, adding, "Dae ye fancy a fish supper?"

I replied in the affirmative and my visitor shuffled off into the night while I stamped my feet and pushed my hands further into my greatcoat pockets keeping the cane tightly held under my armpit. I had still about twenty minutes to do before the next guard took over, when out of the gloom the voice said, "Get that intae ye!" and pushed a hot newspaper bundle into my hand as he hurriedly moved off into the night. I jammed the supper into my coat pocket and dined like a lord while the hot parcel sent a warm glow into the side of my half-chilled body. The delicacy did not require a knife and fork either. I have often wondered if my mysterious benefactor is still alive, for I want to repay him. As the saying goes: I owe him one!

As food, and sometimes the lack of it, has a strong influence in one's memory, it was interesting to recall how we augmented our limited army diet, which was unimaginative and very dull. The local baker, Mason's, used to position his delivery van on the street opposite the main hall as we returned from a fifteen minute PT jog, held religiously every morning (in the dark) around 6 a.m., after the duty piper had wakened us to the strains of 'Hey Johnny Cope, Are Ye Wauken Yet?'. We cursed the piper as we paraded in vests and shorts, but we always bought two rolls from the baker's van when dismissed after parade. We then washed, shaved and got dressed for breakfast of porridge and perhaps a rasher of streaky bacon.

Often on a Friday evening a few of us went along to Mason's upstairs tearooms and ordered steak and kidney pie, peas, bread and butter and tea, which cost us one shilling each.

The other take-away food outlet was Henderson's chip cart, it could always be spotted by the volumes of coal-black smoke belching from its short chimney, the wee horse resting between the shafts. Unfortunately the fat in the pan was not always hot enough and the customers were served soggy, greasy chips flavoured with smoke from the inefficient firing system — especially when there was a swirling wind at some draughty street corner.

As winter dragged towards mid-December, the battery was entrained at Selkirk Railway Station for our next move which returned us to Kilmarnock where we billeted in the Grand Halls, in a somewhat better-organised environment. No sooner had we arrived when there was a heavy snowfall, followed by a request from the LMS railway company for volunteers to dig out three sections of railway wagons buried in drifts just a short distance beyond Old Cumnock on the main Kilmarnock-London line. We armed ourselves with shovels, scarves and Balaclavas. The railway company promised us a hot meal. As soon as we arrived we got stuck in and worked with a determined will. It was hard work and we gradually got wet, which in turn made us feel cold and miserable. As time dragged on we anxiously waited for a dining car to arrive, as a hot meal would have boosted our morale. Our enthusiasm started to wane so we downed tools and contacted a signal-box attendant who telegraphed our request for the promised hot meal. There was a prolonged delay before a signal stated that food was on its way. The boys returned to work and after another disappointing long delay, a pilot engine arrived with bare bread-and-jam sandwiches and urns of half-cold tea!

The men threw away their shovels and demanded to be taken back to Kilmarnock, arriving there just after 4 p.m. Having had nothing substantial to eat since a very early morning breakfast, and being soaked to the skin, cold and hungry, the local men were sent home for hot baths and dry clothing, and told to report back for muster parade next morning. LMS railways were left to finish the job themselves without unpaid and unfed army labour. The job involved using three steam locos as one unit with a huge snowplough up front. They would gather momentum and physically ram the snow, packing it solid between the deep cuttings. We would then 'cast' the snow by shovelling it out of the way, gradually clearing the wagons, which were then dragged out by the engines to a siding along the track.

Training was stepped up and routemarches kept us fit during the long-drawn-out winter. There was trouble in Norway, but the British troops could not hold on and we had no fighting equipment to go anywhere, so the first winter was stalemate and it was lucky for us that we lived on an island. The war seemed a long way off for us. Though we did have some troops over in France, it was mainly 'all quiet on the Western Front'.

By the end of March 1940 the worst of winter was beginning to recede, leaving us still with a lot of icy winds and rain. However, rumour now had it that a big move was afoot and we started to pack ready for whatever was to eventuate. We had been doing extensive routemarches to keep us fit and orders were given to move out. A long, winding column of troops marched from Kilmarnock, again in an easterly direction, followed by a few commandeered baggage trucks. The troops marched up the Irvine Valley and headed for Lanarkshire, stopping every hour for a ten-minute rest break, as prescribed in King's Regulations and strictly adhered to throughout the British Army. The route passed by Loudoun Hill and Drumclog, and this time we were not turning back. We camped out in the cold, wet, frozen fields, sleeping in our uniforms, two men to a makeshift bivouac made up by binding two rubber capes together and using trimmed branches as props. It was a primitive and arduous experience with hail sometimes falling during the night. Our feet were numb and we tried to sleep with our heads covered inside the rolled blankets, our breath being used as a recycling heating agent. Ice formed inside the crude mini-tent which had no walls and the only ventilation came from crudely laced end flaps held together with binder twine. Having a freezing cold wash out in the open fields was no picnic either, coupled with unwashed feet, blistered inside sweat-saturated socks!

However, we soldiered on through Lanarkshire and found ourselves marching through Peebles. While stopped by the roadside in Innerleithen main street, a kind woman bought some buns, etc. from a baker's van across the road and handed them out to the hungry, leg-weary troops. I was given a doughnut while another lady poured out sweet milky tea from an oversize kettle; Border hospitality was catching up with us once more.

After camping overnight just beyond Walkerburn, the column moved on and turned right at Caddonfoot, marching over the Yair Bridge along the Linglie Road to Selkirk. The Auld Toon stood sentinel across the Ettrick Valley. The pipes and drums could be heard by the people of Selkirk as the long column of men came into view where the road winds its way towards the Linglie Farm. The regiment camped that night among the trees within the Haining estate where a good meal was provided, and the lads got the night off to visit old friends in a well-loved neighbourhood. It was more like a homecoming to many of us. We had been on the road six days and blisters were commonplace, but we volunteered to march on the next day rather than be picked up by the stragglers' truck.

The final day saw us march through Hawick and on to Stobs Camp, a godforsaken place high on the desolate moors, guaranteed to daunt the hearts of brave men used to hardship. It was more like a prisoner-of-war camp, offering little comfort to the tired and weary foot soldiers of King George VI.

We were only a few days at Stobs when there was a muster parade for all ranks. The CO told us we were to get seven days' leave and I was on the first batch to go due to alphabetical order, travelling all the way back to Kilmarnock where my mother got a pleasant surprise. It seemed silly, marching all the way to Stobs just to get sent home again on leave but no one was complaining and I celebrated my nineteenth birthday during that leave so it was quite a happy coincidence.

I returned from leave to find the regiment at Stobs Camp packing up ready to move. Some had already gone ahead with the advance party — rumour said to Haltwhistle, near Hexham across the Cheviots, but when we entrained at the camp railway station, the slow-moving train kept going south right into the heart of England, which was foreign to us. Most of the Scots lads had never been in England before and joked about passports and customs barriers. The long troop train finally discharged us at Newbury in Berkshire. Our new home was to be in bell tents soaked in creosote and standing off the Hungerford road about two miles out of town. This was on an estate-type farm, which reared oversized pigs penned adjacent to our humble abode. The southern sun was warm and pleasant and, provided the wind was in the right direction, the country air was intoxicating. We fed well and the local bread was round and varied in texture, which added to our acceptance of the English way of life. The boys enjoyed the quaint country pubs and sampled the cider, which was more potent than first thought. I preferred grapefruit juice in those days, but joined in with the lads for the odd good night at the local.

The WVS forces canteen at Newbury had been newly opened and its location was not widely known. Sanny Frew and I strolled along a back street behind the main shopping area where we discovered it by pure accident. We hesitated outside as Sanny and I stared at the heaped plates of sandwiches and buns, etc. There was also a small billiard table and the ladies looked towards us, anticipating their first customers. A chorus of voices invited us in, but we stood embarrassed by the doorway as we had only about tuppence between us and payday was still two days away. I was paid seven shillings per week as I allocated the other seven to my mother; Sanny was in a similar situation. As Sanny had a broad Ayrshire country accent, he amused his audience when trying to explain our predicament. Without more ado we were ushered in and served with sandwiches and home-made cakes on the house. When asked for an explanation, our hostesses said that they were fascinated by our accents, especially Sanny's! His delivery was slow, droll and guttural, but very sincere. My dialect appeared easier to follow but when told we were from Scotland, none of our new friends had been there so it was an amusing experience for all of us. We stayed till closing time and were given an open invitation to call in as often as we could. Sanny was a big hit with the staff and we enjoyed their kind, genuine hospitality, making sure that we paid our way on the few occasions we managed to return.

Unfortunately our stay in Newbury was too brief, as we received urgent orders to move east. Dunkirk was to be the British Expeditionary Force's last stand prior to evacuation from Europe, and unarmed home units were soon to become the front line of defence.

The regiment entrained at Newbury Station and travelled over to St Albans. From there we transferred to coaches, which circuited Greater London then went as far as Great Dunmow in Essex. We split up from there, and our troop moved on to a small village called Stebbing just off the main Braintree road.

The situation in France was hopeless and Dunkirk was being evacuated. Invasion was imminent as we stood to at dawn and again at dusk waiting for enemy parachutists. We were now Britain's first line of defence, covering the beaches and waterways along the south-eastern seaboard of England. Although we were an artillery unit, all we possessed were hurriedly issued Canadian Ross .303 rifles, covered initially in thick grease, and five rounds of ammunition, later increased to one small cardboard box containing about twenty rounds, bulging in our battledress map pocket. We stood to by the corner of the fields and along the hedgerows, waiting, looking skyward to the east like the wise men of Bethlehem, only for a very different purpose.

After a brief spell at Stebbing, we moved over to Brightlingsea, east of Colchester and were billeted at a country house just out of town. This was our new HQ. It was there we received our first fifteen-hundredweight Ford V8 trucks. The signallers took over the Martello tower and scanned the sea and air for possible enemy movement. A phone line ran from the pier underwater to Mersea Island.

Unfortunately, the submarine cable was fouled by a dredger clearing the main channel. Two of us were told to trace the fault. It was around midnight when we tried to commandeer the only available dinghy at the jetty, but the RN sailor was reluctant to part with his boat until his commander arrived from somewhere in town. Their ship was anchored out in the Colne estuary so we had to wait for his return. On his arrival, the RNVR officer heartily agreed not only to lend us his dinghy, but that he and his AB would act as crew. First we rowed over to his ship where the commander left a few instructions and collected two grappling hooks, then it was down to business.

The only light was the glint from the sea water as the oars dipped. The night was calm but overcast. We had to feel our way in the dark as we dragged the hooks through the black, slimy mud. The two ends were finally located and a new section was joined in, both waterproof joints made in almost total darkness by touch and instinct.

The commander then invited us back to the ship for supper and hoped his cook had carried out his instructions. We climbed aboard the peacetime luxury cruiser, seconded to the Admiralty by the owner, now commander of his own ship. The aroma from the galley was something one does not experience ashore and the delicacy placed before us was a dream to behold: fresh-caught lemon sole cooked to perfection in pure butter with all the trimmings. It was a fitting end to a most trying and arduous night's work. Rule Britannia.

Still covering the same coastline, our troop moved round to St Osyth where we were 'attacked' by a newly formed commando unit at a farm just before the village. They tried to 'steal' our equipment as part of a training exercise, with blackened faces and hunting knives between their teeth.

A telegram arrived informing me that my father had died after a long illness, and I left almost immediately for home, travelling through London at the height of an air raid. Bombs were crashing around us as we waited for the Glasgow train, delayed until the all-clear sounded. The tube stations were crowded with people preparing to bed down for another night in comparative safety, while tea trolleys served hot drinks and sandwiches. While at St Osyth, my mate Bob and I went out one night, sauntered into the village restaurant and ordered two cups of tea. The waitress was puzzled as we wanted nothing to eat. Then the manager came over and sat down at our table. He recognised our Scottish accent, and when he learned we both came from Kilmarnock asked if we knew how to make whisky. We hesitated, and he promptly hailed the waitress, telling us it was on the house as he had already guessed we were both broke. We ordered sausage, egg and chips, bread and butter and a pot of tea. After a good meal and a long chat with *mein host* whom we thanked for his hospitality, with tongue in cheek we left the establishment promising to procure the recipe for Scotch whisky, adding that it could take up to three weeks as we had to write to a friend who worked at the factory. Our host had wanted to make criminals of us, but we had turned the situation to our gastronomical advantage. He kept enquiring about us, but our mates led him to believe we had been posted or were away on a course. Meanwhile, Bob and I steered clear of him until F Troop moved on to Clacton-on-Sea where we billeted at John Groom's Crippleage, and we saw our first snow in England.

Our troop had a new BSM posted to us, who claimed to have been at Dunkirk. We were soon to discover that he did not like anyone very much other than himself and was out to throw his weight around, even though he was slight of stature. I later met a soldier who had known him previously and it seems that he left the area three weeks before the Germans arrived.

Bob and I manned the switchboard one cold wintry night, with the usual orders to wake the duty bombardier and cooks for reveille and 'gunfire' respectively. We woke them but both blokes turned over and went back to sleep. It was not found necessary to obtain a signature from them so we had no proof when the BSM charged us with neglecting to obey orders and blamed us for the whole affair. The troop commander was away and his place was taken by a first lieutenant who initially dismissed the charge. However, on the BSM's overbearing insistence we were both 'awarded' seven days' confined to barracks.

Our BSM decided to give us pack drill as well, and there the man's true character emerged. It was a humiliating experience, being innocent on all counts. On hindsight, we should not have accepted the officer's punishment and should have opted for retrial by a higher authority. The senior NCOs were dumbfounded by the WO's vindictive manner and tried to make things easier for us, but the BSM took us on pack drill himself, making us run at the double wearing gas masks and full packs (two) as well as water bottle, rifle and steel helmet, in deep, still-falling snow. Our masks steamed up, causing us to run 'blind' while the sick-minded person jeered at our unwarranted predicament. Only the BSM laughed at his behaviour. The incident was not to be forgotten and he got his desserts from a more aggressive element long afterwards, out east. Authority in the wrong hands is the most dangerous weapon on earth and reflects a deep mental instability.

At Clacton, while servicing their searchlight during daylight on the promenade, a lone German plane spotted the crew while their lens pointed skywards. The beam acted as a homing beacon, the plane dived to attack and scored a direct hit on the luckless crew. The lesson was noted by all searchlight batteries and the dangerous practice was stopped immediately.

## Clacton — 1940-41:

The snow melted, and as the weather improved the battery deployed inland, linking up with other units in a three-day exercise. Our equipment was limited and we still awaited badly needed guns and vehicles. The British Army had lost everything in Belgium and France during the retreat to Dunkirk. We had to start all over again. Morale was high in spite of being very much on our own. All Europe was forced to capitulate and the United States remained neutral, although they were prepared to lend-lease obsolete World War One equipment to their gallant English 'Kinfolk', making a 'fast buck' as a sideline. All our gold reserves were shipped to Fort Knox as collateral, and as far as I know it is still there to this day! Britain had never been invaded in almost 900 years and we took our losses in our stride. From then on it was to be blood, sweat and tears, as Winston Churchill put it.

Meanwhile, during those three days of manoeuvres, I was told to report back to base and collect all my gear as I had been posted to an undisclosed destination. I got a pillion ride back with the dispatch rider who delivered the signal. On arrival at Battery HQ I only had enough time to grab a sandwich and a mug of tea before I was handed a rail warrant and ordered to report to Colchester Barracks.

On arrival, I found about twenty other blokes standing outside an office, and asked someone what was happening. Then we were all directed over to a temporary office hut inside the barracks perimeter. It had a door marked 'private', and we stood around in groups outside waiting to be called. The first man went in, there was a long pause, then the door opened and out came a grim-faced soldier. We all looked at him expectantly, but he said nothing as he walked away. Number two went in and later emerged with his face ashen white. No comment. Then my name was called and I thought, 'here goes'. I was very calm. I stood to attention and smartly saluted the colonel seated at the table in front of me. He had a patch over one eye and was wiry in build. He was certainly not a young man and looked more like a hook-nosed hatchetman than an officer in the British Army!

He glanced up at me and barked, "Name, rank and number?" Then more softly, "Age? Married or single? Qualifications? Sports? Other interests? Swim? Navigate? Next of kin? Religion?" Whatever he had in mind, I seemed acceptable to him. He then asked, "Any questions?"

I quietly said "Yes," and demanded to know the reason for the interview and was I on a charge.

His voice changed as he told me it was all very hush-hush. He was forming a commando unit and all personnel had to be A1-plus (medically), preferably single, and conversant with map reading and signals. They would soon teach me to swim and, after training, we would hide away somewhere doing the odd raid on Norway, Holland or France, was I interested?

"Definitely not!" was my bold reply.

"Then why did you volunteer?" he asked.

That's what puzzled me too: it must have been our sergeant major, who did want rid of me, but I was not ready to go anywhere. I explained the situation and apologised for wasting his time. He accepted but swore me to secrecy, then allowed me to leave on that assurance. I quietly left the room tight lipped, scrounged a meal at the barracks cookhouse, then hitched a lift back to Battery HQ. The BSM was surprised to see me. As I told the troop commander I was unsuitable, he simply said, "Hard luck, Sergeant Major; welcome back, Signaller."

The unit moved up to Dovercourt, situated between Harwich and Parkeston Quay naval base. All civilian personnel had been evacuated except those on essential war work. The men were billeted in empty semi-detached council-type houses in a street which ran parallel to the main road into Harwich.

One day an unexploded aerial torpedo became lodged deep in the ground down the street from us. The bomb disposal squad had a tricky job on their hands, and all electric power was cut off during the emergency.

During the power cut 1 was asked to help start an old 1927 six-wheeled Morris which had just been delivered. The sergeant told me to swing the handle while he set the throttle and ignition. I grabbed the handle and gave it an almighty swing, the motor kicked back violently and I was left with a broken wrist. I reported to the nearest first-aid post, but due to the power cut could not have it X-rayed. My arm was put in a splint and I was told to report to my own MO at Manningtree the following morning as it was now late evening. I suffered the severe pain all night and finally saw my MO who gave me two aspirins and sent me on to Colchester Military Hospital. The right arm was X-rayed and the fracture confirmed, but all the wards were full up. The major (a Scot) told me not to worry as he would have it fixed in next to no time. He fixed it all right — without an anaesthetic, and nearly sent me through the roof. My arm was then put in plaster and I returned to Dovercourt the same evening.

On my return, I was told that it was later discovered the old truck had its own electric starter, which was in good working order. Lesson number two: never grip the handle with the thumb over it.

During the night of gale-force winds some barrage balloons broke loose, dragging their steel cables across the countryside, and played havoc with the high-tension grid lines. We could only watch helplessly as bright flashes lit the night sky.

Our stay at Dovercourt coincided with the ripening of the victoria plums growing in several orchards, through which by sheer good luck our field telephone lines passed. The lines were well patrolled by signals-section 'volunteers' who classed it as a 'plum' job, and the battledress blouse was used to its full advantage.

The regiment moved again. This time we occupied an area just north and east of Saxmundham in Suffolk. Battery HQ was located in Westleton, and our guns were now 75mm World War One French field guns. We occupied a wooded copse just up the road. While at Westleton (Suffolk), where we were stationed over an extended period, a number of incidents took place, of which I will mention but a few. Firstly, we had been bombed by a returning Dornier which had jettisoned its cargo of incendiaries across the heath in front of our gun positions. We were dug in and camouflaged round the perimeter of a pine copse situated on higher ground. There was a solitary house in the centre of the resulting heath fire, and our lads gallantly rescued a mother and daughter trapped by the smoke and flames. No real damage was done and the fire was eventually put out.

One day we were lined up beside our trucks (out in the open) and were duly inspected by the brigade commander of the RA. He stopped and asked me about my crossed flags on my arm; regarding promotion, had I any ambition and did I like the army? Well, I was brought up to tell the truth, so I did just that, stating that if it was as easy to get out, as it was to volunteer, I would not be speaking to him right then! I had to give my name and number, was charged and duly 'awarded' seven days' CB (just for answering a direct question)!

The Salvation Army mobile canteen used to visit us occasionally and we were rationed to a small bar of chocolate and ten Churchman No. 10 cigarettes. I didn't smoke in those days, so let one of the lads have them. They told me they were horrible, but they still smoked them!

I was sent to Wakefield Priory, in Yorkshire, on a five-week transport course. I was the only gunner there, all the rest were senior NCOs and officers — thirty-six of us all told. Four passed with distinction, including myself, and Major 'Goldie' Gardiner, the CO (and an MG racing-driver), requested I be transferred to his training battery as an instructor. However I was turned down flat by my own CO, who refused to allow my subsequent promotion on the grounds that I was "too valuable to him as a signaller"!

I was very disappointed and said so, but I was simply told to forget the whole incident. I was doomed to be a signaller for the duration.

Each week, if we were lucky, Bob and I went into Ipswich on the duty truck with a day pass which involved a 'bath parade' (whether we needed it or not!). After visiting the public baths, we went round to Lyons Coffee Shop and had a meal (usually bangers and mash followed by apple turnover and custard) — a treat for us. Bob would put on the air of a connoisseur and catch the eye of an elderly manageress, who would be persuaded to make us a 'special' pot of white coffee which was delicious! She knew we were a bit far from home. We'd usually proceed to a large cinema with a real cinema organ, which fascinated me as I'd never seen one before. While the organist played, sheet music with their lyrics was screened and a white ball bounced across the words as we all joined in singing 'Run Rabbit, Run Rabbit, Run, Run, Run', or some other pop song of the day.

On the way home to Westleton after boarding the duty truck (Ford V8, 30-cwt with its canvas canopy) we'd all sing parochial favourites, prompted by the lads from all corners of the British Isles: 'Ilkla Moor Baht 'At', 'Blaydon Races', 'Any Old Iron', 'Blackpool by the Sea', 'Scotland For Ever', and many more uncensored versions.

The driver had to circumnavigate numerous roadblocks, driving with masked headlamps, and occasionally went up a farm road by mistake.

One night we were both starving of hunger, the rest had all turned in and all was dead quiet around the Nissen hut in the centre of the wood. Bob and I sneaked over to the dining tent to forage for grub and found part of a loaf of bread on the serving table beside an open seven-pound tin of raspberry jam with a fair amount still left in the bottom. We hacked off a couple of slices in the dark and spread the jam liberally on the bread, then sneaked back to the darkened billet. We enjoyed every mouthful. Next morning when lining up for breakfast, I noticed the jam tin still there and casually looked inside, the bottom was a solid mass of dead wasps! No wonder the cook didn't lock it up in the cookhouse the night before! On hindsight, the jam was a bit crunchy.

We took turns at manning a cliff-top observation pillbox just south of Dunwich village, and kept a constant watch across the mined beaches towards coastal convoys under escort dragging a naval-type barrage balloon to deter dive bombers. We were supposed to mess with the Cameronians nearby, but an arrogant CSM yelled at us like dogs so we withdrew from the arrangement and fed ourselves at the dugout. It was there we noticed how infantry privates were treated like scum, decent blokes they were too, and fellow countrymen (15th Scottish Division).

While down at battery HQ in Westleton village, the Signals billet adjoined a private mansion separated by a fence, and we were attracted by the apple orchard which stood between the house and the road. I never saw such beautiful eating apples growing in Britain; they looked like Red

Delicious with a pinkish flesh. The temptation was strong but Bob and I decided to approach the owner. We knocked on the front door of his house and waited. Soon there was a scuffle and someone was cursing at guard dogs straining at the leash! The door opened and there, standing before us were two huge mastiffs and a slim, medium-built, middle-aged man who scowled at us and demanded to know our business. Undaunted, I asked if we could have some apples, which we offered to buy if necessary. He replied by stating they no longer were sent to London fruit markets but he would rather let them rot on the trees than give us any. He then warned us off his property and threatened to unleash the dogs on us! By hell, here was an enemy towards the troops, which he so obviously detested, but we politely withdrew.

Later, Bob and I agreed that we had no other alternative, so that night we climbed the fence and dropped into the orchard armed with two sandbags. There was no moon and all was calm and still with a slight frost. I climbed a selected tree and gently dropped some apples down to Bob. Suddenly dogs started growling inside the house, but we kept on collecting. A man yelled at them to keep quiet, but they persisted. Eventually, the door was unbolted and I whispered to Bob to clear off which he discreetly did. Unfortunately, the owner emerged outside along with another man too quickly and shouted, "There's someone at the apples!" He unleashed the dogs, which bounded down to my tree and snarled away at the trunk. My eyes were accustomed to the darkness and I froze motionless in a still-life pose, straddled across the upper main branches. The two men came down from the house. One said it was a pity that they couldn't shine a torch because of the blackout regulations. It was then decided we must have scarpered. I heard all this while suspended just above them, waiting while the dogs kept clawing at the tree trunk. Eventually they slowly retired to the house and locked up for the night between 11.30 p.m. and midnight. I stuffed my XO's battledress blouse with apples and calmly returned to the billet, triumphant!

A few days later I went home on leave to Kilmarnock, and my mother thought I had bought the apples — a rare treat in wartime. Sometimes it is best not to tell a mother everything.

Before going on leave on one occasion, Bob offered to crease my best trousers — a nice gesture which I accepted. He turned them inside out, dampened the fold and then lined the inside with cookhouse soap. The trousers were then carefully folded and placed between two sheets of cardboard under my bedding (we had no mattresses or pyjamas in our outfit). Next morning early I got dressed and was soon on my long journey home. During the trip it rained somewhere along the way and as my trousers got damp my knees started to nip a bit then gradually got worse! I learned a valuable lesson that day but had to keep them on till I got home many hours later, then changed into my civvies as usual. My knees were red for days afterwards!

Two places stand out in my memory: Selkirk and Westleton. It was at Selkirk I met my future wife (whom I married after the war in 1946) and where we later settled, allowing me to recuperate from the mental and other scars of war. I found the Selkirk people the friendliest people on earth and greatly admired their quiet and leisurely way of life. The small county town nestles among the Scottish Border hills on the river Ettrick just before it joins the Tweed near Abbotsford, the home of Sir Walter Scott, poet and writer and one-time sheriff (magistrate) of the Royal and Ancient Burgh of Selkirk. The boys often spoke of Selkirk with deep affection. Many continued to receive the odd parcel from Selkirk friends long after we went out east. We often linked the two places singing 'South of the Border down Westleton Way'.

## *Prepare to Move:*

As the war dragged on, the Germans 'allowed' our armament factories to get into full production and our civilian counterparts were really putting everything into it. Trucks, guns and aircraft were now rolling off the assembly lines in ever-increasing numbers. The British Nation was united as never before in those darkest days of the war when we were to stand alone as champions of the free world. As always, the British Commonwealth closed ranks and stood beside us as our family of nations. In times of adversity your real friends come forward while others wait to join the potential victors, cashing in on the hapless victims.

It was now the Autumn of 1941 and the regiment finally took delivery of twenty-four 25-pounder guns/howitzer artillery guns along with a fleet of Ford V8 4x4 quad tractors and six Bren-carriers, known as armoured OPs and fitted with No. 11 wireless transmitters. We were now in business at long last. Then it was down to Larkhill artillery range on Salisbury Plain. The guns were calibrated and we fired gas shells as well as HE (high explosive), AP (armour piercing) and smoke shells. It had taken two years to get fully equipped and the army finally declared the 130th Field Regiment ready for overseas duty. We moved up to Gateshead (Newcastle) just before Christmas 1941 and were given five days' embarkation leave. The big moment came at long last.

The vehicles and guns were loaded at Liverpool and we entrained at Newcastle for an unknown destination. The long troop train travelled through the cold and dark January night bypassing the bigger towns, and then headed west, finally stopping in a huge marshalling yard. It was foggy so I stuck my head out of the carriage window and asked a plain-clothes man where we were. He replied in a Glasgow accent, "You mind your ain business, Mac!" I smiled: it was Parkhead, in the heart of Glasgow. Finally the train crawled into Shieldhall Dock and we stopped alongside the *Strathmore*.

We slipped downstream next day and anchored in the Clyde estuary, better known to all Scotsmen as the 'Tail of the Bank', where the convoy began to form up for the coming voyage. About half the ships had loaded at Liverpool, and we rounded the Mull of Kintyre into the heavy swell of the mighty Atlantic Ocean about the 10th January, 1942. The P&O ship *Strathmore* led the convoy and we were escorted part of the way by the battle cruiser *Resolution* and a varying number of destroyers and corvettes. Our ship was the commodore's flagship and all signals emanated from it to all ships under his command, including the Royal Navy escorts.

One night during a routine change in course, *Resolution*, sailing alongside, failed to alter helm and continued on a collision course towards *Strathmore*. Our ship suddenly took evasive action, causing it to almost heel right over, and we were thrown against the bulk heads. It was night-time; all the lights went out and we all thought we'd been hit. Gradually the ship righted herself and the lights came on again. We later learned that the *Resolution* missed us by only a few feet. A court of enquiry was held later and there were a few red faces in the Royal Navy that day. Someone had failed to obey the change signal, consequently *Strathmore* nearly lost a few barnacles!

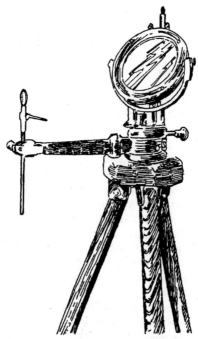

*Heliograph and Tripod*

### Destination Burma:

Bob Picken was a professional barber with no one to cut his hair so he taught me the business as my broken wrist needed the therapy anyway. We later formed a partnership, nicknamed by the boys 'Sweeney Todd & Company'. There was never a shortage of customers during our off-duty hours as we had no official barber 'on the strength'. We were expected to put our earnings into the Battery Welfare Fund, but we argued that we would go on strike first, in spite of threats from the BSM.

Soon after we boarded the *Strathmore*, the BSM asked if we had brought our clippers with us as there were no other barbers on board and there was estimated to be 5,000 haircuts to attend to. The severe Atlantic gales lasted four days and it was down to business when we reached calmer waters. From then on we cut hair on the main-deck every day. Our clients sat on wooden boxes procured from the galley. We charged our lads fourpence and all other units sixpence. The officers paid above the minimum rate as they were travelling first class. The duty officer of the day collected our earnings and deposited them with the purser, duly receipted. We spent a few bob at the ship's dry canteen while our mates either manned the ack-ack guns or carried out deck duties as detailed. There was always a card school going on during the evenings, down below in the mess decks.

Most of us slept on deck, weather permitting, lulled to sleep by the gentle motion of the ship as the stars appeared to sway in the heavens high above us. It all seemed so unreal. For all we knew there could have been an enemy sub lurking in our path ahead, but our luck held until one sad incident when a Focke-Wulf long-range bomber, operating from Dakar in north-west Africa, attacked a freighter which had sustained engine trouble and had just dropped behind having been ordered to make for Gibraltar. The escort ships rushed to her aid as volumes of smoke could be seen far astern. The ship was abandoned as she was doomed. How many were saved is hard to say but there were some survivors. The convoy sailed on south then hove to off Freetown long enough to refuel and take on water from lighters.

The troops were entertained by the natives offering fruit for sale, sending the goods up in baskets, while others dived down into the clear water for coins.

The convoy was anchored inside the boom-defence area and was relatively safe until we continued our journey south. The weather was good and a fast pace was maintained. I observed the derrick-like masts of an American warship just over the horizon, but we each continued on course. Half the convoy broke off when we rounded the Cape of Good Hope. They headed for Cape Town while our lot continued east and north for Durban, which was a beautiful sight to behold as we had been at sea for four long weeks confined to cramped quarters like sardines. We lived well below the main decks while the officers lived in proper cabins and dined in a civilised manner, waited upon by stewards, using the ship's silver as on a cruise ship in peacetime. We envied them, but in war some have to make more sacrifices than others and we were treated accordingly — as the French say *"C'est la guerre!"*

Our newly accumulated wealth from hair cutting had stumbled on one snag: we were advised that paper currency was not acceptable in South Africa, so Bob and I settled for silver and went down the gangway each day weighted down with our loot, only to return skint at night. We dined only in the best restaurants, took in a few shows, toured the sights, did a bit of shopping and bought a new set of hair clippers each as ours were almost worn out. We rounded off the spree by each purchasing a new wristwatch. We went into one shop where the Afrikaner refused British currency. His arrogance made us believe he could be a Nazi! Our boys annoyed the whites by pulling the Zulus about in their rickshaws and having their pictures taken beside the highly feathered and colourful 'warriors' of the South African veldt.

We sailed from Durban after three and a half days. Our orders were to head for Bombay as Singapore had fallen and Burma was overrun by the Japanese, who appeared to be invincible. Our depleted convoy was now in an enemy submarine zone where they were operating off Madagascar. We had one scare and our escorts began dropping depth charges while the convoy broke formation and increased speed. There were no further incidents and we reached Bombay safely.

Old regular soldiers had told some fascinating tales about India; now it was our turn to find out for ourselves. This was the land of Gunga Din made famous by Kipling who knew what he was on about, as was proved to us later. We were to learn the hard way through blood, sweat and tears — Churchill was right for once.

On arrival at Bombay we entrained immediately for Deolali where it was very hot. The grub was all fresh food and we all queued up for seconds. There were also fresh oranges and bananas, grapes and watermelons, etc. Our duties at Deolali included guarding the baggage train down at the military railway siding, as India is famous for the 'loose wallahs' who earn a lucrative living by thieving and selling.

All was quiet during my turn on guard patrol where a constant vigil was maintained along the line of wide-gauge railway wagons. Suddenly I spotted a turbaned Sikh civilian in his mid-twenties hovering hesitantly at the yard entrance. As I approached he stood his ground. When I asked his reason for being there, he replied that he wished to tell my fortune! I laughed out loud and attempted to send him on his way, but he persisted. I had to admire his clean and tidy appearance, which revealed a sincerity in his dignified defiance. The Sikh was careful not to cross the open gateway but objected to my "insulting and disbelieving attitude". He struck me as a young man of substance and not to be treated as an enemy. I therefore tried to explain my attitude towards fortune-tellers by saying he could believe what he liked, but that I was also entitled to my scepticisms. He also wanted a fee for his services but I was adamant that it should end right there, and said so! As he made to turn away, my remarks must have irked him badly, he snarled back to me, grabbed my free hand, and muttered, "Something to prove I'm not a fraud." He glanced momentarily at my palm as I pulled my hand away, and calmly said, "You will be in a very dangerous situation where many of your comrades will die very badly — but you will survive."

I knew it could well happen, perhaps in action somewhere, but that was pure conjecture. I sent the fortune-teller away with a flea in his ear.

He yelled back, "I don't tell lies, you'll see I'm right." But it did happen, nine months later.

While at Deolali, I became ill and was taken to hospital with gastric influenza, and on the following day, the regiment moved east towards Bengal, somewhere beyond Calcutta. I was starved in hospital for three weeks but finally I was given some money and put on a train to Calcutta where I had a tooth removed by a civilian dentist, whom I gladly paid five rupees.

There were no lines of communications set up as yet and any units moving into the Bengal area had to fend very much for themselves. Such was the way things were in our part of the world. This was to be the state of affairs for a long time to come. We were later to be dubbed 'The Forgotten Army' — XIV (the 14th).

I finally rejoined the unit, which was camped near the main wide-gauge railway line miles from nowhere. I was told to report to the battery commander as soon as I arrived and he welcomed me like a long lost son. I was very weak, pale and very thin. The BC said he was determined to hold on to me as I could have been Y-listed. This meant any personnel away from his unit through sickness for more than three weeks could be posted to any other unit requiring replacements, as his previous regiment forfeited the right to reclaim him. I was told to get all the rest I could as I was excused all duties for three months if necessary. He was a true gentleman and I was by his side when he died fatally wounded on the 4th January, 1943. He gave his final instructions to a brother officer concerning his wife and family. He knew it was all over and showed what a courageous soldier and husband he was. I was proud to have served with Major William Breckinbridge from Irvine in Ayrshire, Scotland.

We moved across the Ganges/Brahmaputra Delta to Comilla where I celebrated my twenty-first birthday. My mates bought some spuds and watermelons from the natives nearby and we polished them off with a tin of bully beef. It was dark early that evening as we sat round the campfire, which was reflected in dozens of pairs of eyes hungrily staring at us from the surrounding scrub. It was a pack of wild dogs, which were common in those parts. We were too hungry ourselves to invite them to the party as the army had not yet caught up with us regarding rations. Officers had to forage locally with limited funds and buy whatever was available. No doubt this caused the locals to do with less, consequently forcing prices to rise, much to the detriment of the very poor natives.

Our troop moved down the metre-gauge railway branch line to Noakhali, situated on the northern tip of the Bay of Bengal. This was to be our home for the next few months. The gunners built gun positions and erected walls and roofs around them to look like bungalows from the sea. The climate was very hot and humid. At high tide the ground was almost awash, and the place was infested with swarms of mosquitoes, flying ants and large winged beetles, which chilled the sweat down the back of your spine during our all-night vigil wearing headphones at the telegraph transmitter.

Bob and I were dive bombed as we maintained the only link with the outside world. We worked a two-man shift as no one else was available. Competent signallers were hard to come by, so we had to do four hours on and four hours off, day and night for weeks on end without a break. We stopped cutting hair in protest as we were exhausted; the troop commander was displeased.

One night, about two in the morning, we received a ciphered message which I assisted the troop commander to decode. It was a red alert of a possible attack. An Indian company supporting us about five miles behind to the north adjoining the railway, was not answering the telegraph, so I was dispatched to raise the alarm in a pitch-black night along a narrow foot track flanked by thick jungle undergrowth on a motorbike. I had to use a masked headlight and visibility was limited. There were all sorts of nocturnal creatures flying or crawling about on either side of the track, when suddenly I came across a 'log' lying across my path. I stopped and on closer scrutiny saw an animal like a crocodile about five-feet long. I could not turn round on the V-ridge track, so I revved the engine, sounded the horn and yelled, partly out of fright. My helmet was being pushed up by my hair which was standing on end! The animal woke up lazily and staggered into the undergrowth. If it was not a croc, it was the biggest iguana I ever saw anywhere. I proceeded on my way and finally reached the company perimeter where I was challenged by a nervous sentry who took me to his company office.

I was escorted to the company commander's basha and waited while he got dressed before being taken to the duty-signaller, who was fast asleep. At first glance he should have been court martialled, but the poor sod had no one to relieve him as he was the only one who could read Morse. I understood the situation better than most and pleaded his case. Signallers are the unsung heroes and are too often taken for granted by the rank and file. Not everyone can be a fully qualified signaller, as one must acquire a willingness to learn plus an ability to adapt to a new concept — namely the Morse code. A similar comparison would be a good musician learning to read and write music.

Unknown to us, the red alert turned out to be a false alarm — someone had pushed the panic button. I returned to the unit without further incident.

There were a few local riots at Noakhali caused by mischievous rumours that coolies employed by the army were not to be paid, but as it happened, the money was unavoidably delayed by about one day while we waited for the local bank to procure the cash. Coolie labourers were paid daily, hence the misunderstanding.

It was interesting to watch the pay out on such occasions: firstly all the gangs lined up in groups of ten by the roadside and the solemn procedure began. Our duty officer would hand each person one rupee. He would be followed by one of us as escort. The ganger brought up the rear in turn and he took the rupee from the recipient then handed each in turn eight annas (half a rupee). Anyone who complained was not re-engaged next morning and children were included in the gangs of ten, most of whom were related. Graft was the name of the game.

I was also reported for being on a mosque roof with my boots on but countered by asking the high priest if he would have treated a Japanese soldier in the same way. I had been erecting a signalling lamp for the guns to use as an aiming point, to be operated by remote control. The troop commander reprimanded me as a matter of diplomacy — we differed slightly over religious matters.

Our next move was south by rail to Chittagong, which was to become our home until we moved down the Arakan Peninsula prior to Christmas 1942.

Chittagong was almost deserted except for the local natives. The Europeans and rich merchants had fled to safety from the 'imminent' Japanese takeover, which did not eventuate. Cars were left abandoned in the streets and some bungalows still had their radios left on which pointed to a hurried departure by their occupants. When we took over, the bar at the European Club was well stocked with liquor and the uniformed staff were ready to serve us, dressed in their turbans and sashes as usual. There were billiard tables and tennis courts at our behest and horse-drawn gharris to take us back to our billets in the evening.

This mode of living was short lived and very smartly it was 'as you were'. It was suddenly 'officers only' and Britannia ruled the waves once more. The only thing was, we had no navy in that whole area as was proved to our sorrow the following year during the first campaign when we had our backs to the sea down the Arakan Peninsula and not a ship in sight!

Our troop was stationed down river just off the road which followed the branch railway as far as the airfield. We were at the old jute mill surrounded by paddy fields and scrub. During the monsoon season, the flooded paddies were infested with grass snakes which wriggled around our ankles when the signallers had to go out on line patrol.

On one occasion we took a truck across country as one of our lads had been bitten by a snake. The ground was saturated and the track was rutted and treacherous. We finally picked up our patient and proceeded by another route to Chittagong Hospital. It was a race against time and the truck had to be manhandled most of the way until we hit the hard concrete road on the outskirts of the town itself. The gunner survived the ordeal: we got him to hospital with only twenty minutes to spare. It was a poisonous bite. We were to learn that two teeth marks were fatal if untreated while six marks were safe.

Our billets were stifling at night as we were situated on low-lying ground below road level and surrounded by near swamp-like conditions due to the paddy fields. It was a brick building, which housed machinery, and no provision had been made for through ventilation. The place was infested with mosquitoes so we had to use our nets, which made the atmosphere even more stifling. We had to lie naked with just a towel across our middle. Elbows touching the inside walls of the net were promptly bitten and the constant whining sound of the mossies could be heard till daybreak. Outside the door, cobras nestled in the broken bricks and rubble. Two gunners were told to clear up the rubbish outside and unearthed a cobra which tried to make for cover. One man grabbed it by the tail while his mate ran for a hammer from the quad gun tractor. He quickly returned and hit the snake on the head as the other gunner pulled it from the rubble. That was the end of the cobra, but those lads took quite a risk. I suppose we all tended to be a bit devil-may-care and live dangerously being young and still somewhat untamed. We find in later years that men mature quite suddenly after having been near death several times while engaged in battle. Normally a man does not mature mentally until he reaches the age of twenty-five as can be proved by the traffic accident statistics today.

I was appointed to being the Bren-carrier driver/wireless operator with Bob Picken as my co-pilot. Promotion was not for either of us — we were virtually branded indispensable. It was ironical but true. We were part of a team to remain intact until destiny decreed otherwise, which it did in no uncertain terms. The 'brain' in our command post was a genius turned down from OCTU as unsuitable because he would not fit in with the establishment. Many envied the man's mathematical brain, but he did not look like officer material. He was also a brilliant pianist and had postponed his finals at Glasgow University to the legal profession. I was one of his father's pupils at Kilmarnock Technical College, studying the theory of engineering. We called his father Professor. Our command post genius was often 'busted' from lance sergeant to bombardier because he was not arrogant, foul mouthed, or tough enough with his fellow men, a prerequisite handed down from regular army doctrine. When our forefathers were peasants and semi-literate the old guard fought to maintain the status quo. One of our staff sergeants, a regular, could not read or write his own daily routine orders when acting as BSM. The office clerk or duty signaller had to write down his dictation. That is gospel.

The army received a shipload of mules from South America. While at Chittagong, they were graded and allocated to various units. The animals were still wild and frightened and I did not envy the lads who were to handle them. The biggest of the mules were issued to the screwgunners, officially known as mountain-artillery batteries. Their guns were transported in sections and assembled on site. Wheels and gun-barrels, etc. were strapped on the backs of reliable mules, otherwise should a mule decide to go walkabout the guns would be useless, of course.

I do remember places where mules could not negotiate and we became the packhorses. We had to extend ourselves beyond the limits of acceptable human endurance while suffering from malnutrition and lack of sleep. When the legs buckle from utter exhaustion, then total collapse, you know you have done your best.

Chittagong was a thriving port before the war and exported mainly tea and jute from a well-constructed wharf which had a hydraulic crane loading system. The latter intrigued me as my old firm in Kilmarnock specialised in hydraulics. The system relied on an adequate water supply fed by gravity from a strategically situated water tower. The power was transferred through rams which acted like pistons in order to operate the lifting cables threaded through geared pulleys.

The town itself had few notable buildings and resembled a frontier-style railhead, unlike the place Alan Ladd operated from when he and twenty other guys captured Burma on their own, Hollywood-style, with camels, elephants and snake charmers among palm-fringed studio props. Our Chittagong was poor, drab and filthy, the roads were strewn with goats, sacred cows and water buffalo, the people were hungry, dressed in rags and begged for backsheesh. The few ponies strapped between the gharris were like death warmed up, ready to collapse with the least resistance, like skeletons covered with grey, wrinkled skin.

There was a soft drink factory and a cinema. The latter was a bamboo-framed barn screened from the outside with bamboo matting. There was a dirt floor and wooden forms to seat the patrons. Everyone ate peanuts which chicos sold throughout the performance, other kids stood behind us wafting small bamboo fans. When they tired, we gave them a hurry-up, but we rewarded them in good fun, and a few annas worked wonders. As the audience left the 'hall', we walked on a solid bed of peanut shells. There were no fire hydrants, etc., so I only hoped the place never caught fire as it would have been a sad affair for the luckless victims.

## The Scavengers:

Each vehicle in the regiment had letters painted on red and blue (artillery) identity plates front and rear. We also had similar-sized plates displaying the divisional or corps insignia. All units could therefore be easily identified in convoy or in the field. My carrier was the forward reconnaissance unit and belonged to F for Freddie Troop which identified us with the letters RF. When I first took over RF at Chittagong, the Bren carrier was showing signs of wear and tear, having been used in Britain before going to India and having sometimes been handled carelessly. The tracks were stretched to their mechanical limits, also the motor was playing up for some obscure reason and had been for some time.

During our stay down river from Chittagong, we serviced and maintained our equipment as each man knew that his life could depend on a high standard of efficiency. I went over every inch of my vehicle and investigated the fault in the V8 motor, housed amidships inside the carrier, which involved unloading most of the equipment in order to remove the side covers exposing the engine-transmission assembly. All jets and points, as well as fuel pump and carburettor were in good nick, but still the trouble persisted. The previous driver reckoned it had a jinx and was glad to hand it over as he had checked everything himself and was still baffled.

Now I was no mechanic but knew the theory of the internal combustion engine and that when the motor continued to flash back in the carburettor she was being starved of fuel. I therefore removed the part-concealed and multi-curved pipe linking the pump to the carburettor and, *voila,* there it was, a flat spot on a hidden bend caused by a clumsy hand when some previous assembling had been carried out.

Bob Picken had been maintaining his No. 11 wireless and other signalling equipment, but volunteered to come with me to the REME workshop in Chittagong as we needed a new set of tracks. The bloke in charge had none, but he pointed to a carrier being cannibalised, standing derelict in the adjoining yard, and told us to help ourselves. We uncoupled the good tracks on the other carrier then dragged it clear with ours, leaving a twin bed of steel links flat on the ground. I then lined up my vehicle facing the replacement tracks then we dropped our old ones to fall in line. Our carrier was rolled forward and the new tracks proved to be what was required. Bob and I had them coupled and adjusted in a very short time. We were not as dumb as some people thought. Our teamwork raised a few eyebrows as we had to be more than just signallers. I then swapped fuel pipes, which were identical, and the motor assumed a new lease of life as we returned to the old jute mill down river.

Next day we decided to give the carrier and wireless a test run. The route continued down river towards the airstrip with a railway track between us and the wide river to our left, while paddy fields and scrub adjoined the opposite side. We travelled at between 10 and 15 mph. Bob maintained contact with base as I kept an eye on the road ahead, which was narrow and peppered with potholes. Suddenly and without warning there was a frightening crash of huge wings and feathers and a splatter of blood all over and inside the open-top vehicle. Something had collided across the top edge and struck the stout copper aerial rod/base assembly. We both got quite a shock, but I managed to pull up ahead without further mishap. We spat feathers and cleaned off the vehicle as best we could then tried to assess what had happened. On retracing our route back to camp, I saw the rotting carcass of a cow being devoured by turkey-sized vultures tearing at the flesh while lesser birds and animals such as wild dogs stood at bay waiting to join the feast. The dogs roamed the area in packs numbering around twenty in any one group. They were part of nature's chain of scavengers, along with the carrion birds, which helped reduce India's appalling high incidence of disease, which was rife everywhere. Our approach along the road had disturbed the vultures causing some to rise into the wind which crossed our path from left to right. Being heavy with food, their ability to fly clear was impaired and some crashed in a sickening mess literally on top of us! The smell was something awful due to their dietary preference.

The people of India have customs wide and varied which are difficult for a Westener to comprehend. Among the various religious castes, most believe in arranged marriages and wife-swapping among close friends and relations as a token of trust. But the most macabre custom was associated with the highest caste: Parsees or Brahmins. This was the practice of funerals where the dead were placed on high towers, leaving the vultures to devour their flesh. Eventually the human bones would fall through a grill platform to the base of the tower. The bones nowadays ultimately dissolve in a pit filled with quicklime.

### Arakan Peninsula — December 1942 (Objective — Akyab):
F Troop had been assembled at the old jute mill midway between Chittagong and the RAF airstrip when finally our orders were received to entrain our 25-pounders and vehicles on board flat-top wagons and move up to Dohazari. This was the railhead, crossing that precarious rail bridge over the Karnaphuli river. We then one by one took our vehicles, etc. over what was a rather primitive ferry, headed south for Cox's Bazaar and followed the beach round Elephant Point as there was no road. The quad gun tractors had to be dug out of the quicksands and winched using the two Bren carriers as anchors. We had already joined up with E Troop, which combined to form the 494 Field Battery. Our journey was partly assisted by steel barges which bridged some tidal creeks towards Maungdaw. We had lined up our guns ready to fire across the estuary when news came through that the Japs had withdrawn from the township. This made our entry uneventful.

31

Shortly after our arrival, I was detailed to 'volunteer' for a recce party, which was to consist of an RE major, and our machine gunner (Basil Haycock) and myself as driver. My carrier was semi-obsolete and I was invited to select the best available from Brigade HQ, which I did, only to be told by the transport havildar that it belonged to the brigadier! I insisted and got the OK from the big chief himself. I tightened up the tracks, filled her up and took off.

Next morning we were shown our map which simply showed the coastline. The remainder was blank, but coloured green with small dots, and simply said, 'uncharted territory believed mangrove swamps'. We set off at dawn. Foul Point was fifty-six miles south. Our mission was to chart out a route, if feasible. The idea was that the brigade would then use Foul Point as a springboard to capture Akyab.

Progress was slow due to the rough and hazardous terrain. We negotiated numerous creeks with the carrier almost standing on its nose going down the drop into the V-shaped nullahs and climbing up the other side on its tail. My two passengers stood clear and helped clear debris out of my way ahead. We camped out in the scrub. I had been at the wheel for sixteen hours and was dead beat. We took turns on guard. The major was first on, then Basil took over, doing my shift also, waking me up with a mug of tea at daybreak. He reckoned I needed the rest for the next day ahead as I was the only one competent to handle the carrier under such conditions. I was pushing the machine far beyond its designed limits and on many occasions it could have somersaulted if I hadn't held it on a wavering balance using the clutch and foot brake with my heel on the throttle at the same time. The carrier crawled through scrub and mud as the need for higher ground clearance became evident when the bottom of the vehicle frequently got suspended on relatively low ridges and stumps, thereby losing traction. I was very much aware of this hazard, but found it impossible to avoid every obstacle. At the end of the war carriers finally appeared, which incorporated double bogies front and rear and improved tiller-type clutch-operated steering, making a marked improvement all round.

The terrain gradually improved as open paddy fields began to spread out towards the distant coastline. Eventually we reached a village inland from the beach known as Indin about halfway to our objective. We were met by a group of very sad but relieved villagers with a notable absence of young people between the ages of ten and thirty. The villagers told us that the Japs had taken them away as coolies and concubines. We gave what we could spare as the Japs had commandeered all food and livestock. In their gratitude, the very old and the very young swarmed round the carrier, picking off every grain of mud and scrub which clogged the bogies and tracks. I took this opportunity to pump in fresh grease and check water and oil levels before making our sad but mutual farewells.

I started up and made a beeline for the beach, crawling through the soft sandy dunes until finally reaching the firm, wet sand. As luck would have it, the tide was just beginning to recede so we made full use of it. The feeling of a vast limitless highway loomed ahead as I worked my way through the wide-gate 'crash' gearbox into top gear, finally building the speed up to 40 mph. I then maintained a subdued whine from the V8 motor while nursing it at just under full throttle. We didn't seem to be moving as the dunes appeared to drift towards our left rear, while the gentle rollers on our right caressed the warm, friendly beach. For a brief moment war was too far away in this unspoilt oceanic paradise.

Several tidal estuaries had to be negotiated. Basil would hop out and wade ahead of the carrier, then I would slip back into top gear as we regained momentum on the firm, wet surface, which also absorbed a high proportion of sound. This was nature's answer to noise levels and, in our case, we had no wish to broadcast our progress either. Our dash south to Foul Point at the end of the Arakan Peninsula was uneventful, and I drove in a standing posture while focusing my eyes on the distant horizon until a cluster of rocks and sand-locked boulders heralded the end of our journey. The major confirmed our position and its suitability as a base site for a planned assault on Akyab Island to the south, in the Bay of Bengal.

Our mission accomplished, we retraced our route but stopped for a brief look at Donbaik Village hidden from the beach, beyond the sand dunes, I brought the carrier abreast of the skyline, alert to any emergency.

### Donbaik — December 1942 (Prior to Christmas):

The Bren carrier nosed up to the top of the sand dunes overlooking Donbaik, which appeared to be uninhabited except for a faint wisp of smoke hovering above the partly-concealed bush-clad bamboo village. Basil placed the Bren gun almost resting on my steel helmet and waited for the order to fire. The major sat to my left holding the Thompson sub-machine-gun, two Lee-Enfield rifles were strapped inside the front bulkhead, the points of the latter projecting above the armour plate. We kept a box of grenades handy should we be counterattacked. I was inside my helmet when Basil opened fire in order to draw a response should the enemy be in hiding. All hell appeared to be let loose as each burst from the Bren-gun shattered my eardrums, amplified through my steel helmet. It seemed as if Basil was using my head as a bipod. Suddenly the major screamed and yelled in panic, "I'm shot! I'm shot!" as blood appeared all over his bare legs. It looked bad at first glance but I soon realised it was only multiple scratches as I wiped my hand across his knees. The trouble arose when Basil swept across the bulkhead, spraying bullets towards the target area. The bullets literally sheared through the top ends of the rifles, cutting them like butter. Unfortunately, the hardwood sheaths were shattered and sharp splinters scattered across the major's bare knees. I was wearing a combination boiler suit at the time and was unhurt. If the bullets had been a faction lower, they would have ricocheted inside our compartment and that would have been the end of us. It was a lucky escape for all concerned.

There was no response from the village, so after a brief pause the major got out of the carrier and told Basil to accompany him with the sub-machine-gun, taking a few grenades with them. I was told to cover them from the carrier with the Bren gun. If there was any shooting I was to go in and rescue them. I lay on top of the carrier and kept an eagle eye on the area immediately in front and around my two companions. They went out of sight for a short time while I remained tense and on full alert. We were far from base and very much on our own. I waited as the seconds ticked by, then both men quietly reappeared. They said the place was deserted, but there were cooking pots still simmering on the smoking embers. I had heard one solitary shot from the foothills just behind the village, but the major hadn't and Basil was not sure but thought he had. I was sure enough but the major did not confirm it on his report. We slipped off the sand dunes back to the firm, wet beach and headed north in the rapidly changing twilight. Soon it was pitch dark but for the faint glint of stars high above in the still tropical sky. My southbound track marks on the sand were still visible. The light from the phosphorous surf on my left added to my line of sight. The journey back was like a flight through space: eerie but exhilarating.

## Return From Donbaik — December 1942:
As we travelled far into the night, the incoming tide eventually forced us to stop and camp above high water in deep, soft sand just below the sand dunes. We had been told to expect a mule team from the Service Corps to meet us with supplies including petrol. One tank was empty, the other showed one inch left on the dipstick (about one gallon), while I now noticed the odd splutter from the motor which suggested dirt or water in the fuel line.

Next morning as I checked the fault, the major blew his stack as the very soft brass banjo-union parted when I tried to unscrew it from the carburettor. The hexagon head remained in the jaws of the spanner, consequently I was unable to clear the filter and the motor refused to keep running. Basil was sent off to get help and I remained behind to guard the vehicle.

A day or two later two REME mechanics arrived with a new banjo union, drilled out the broken one then cleaned out the jets and filters, saying I'd be billed later. It was obvious that when the union had seized with friction and heat, the metal could not withstand the extra tension required to unscrew it. I felt I was to blame, but knew better when I saw the weak grade of brass where it fractured.

The major had told Basil not to return, but the officer's batman arrived instead. He was a tall lanky lad, a lance naik. I felt sorry for him as he had to put up with an ill-tempered boss, who didn't like me much either — the major was anxious to get rid of me. I was told to take the carrier north and report to the 5/8th Punjabs camped near Alethangyaw. I replied that I required more petrol first as the supplies had not arrived, but he refused to listen and threatened me with a court martial. I insisted that if I must go the batman had to accompany me as there was a very wide estuary to cross before Alethangyaw. I reiterated that I had grave doubts about getting across, but my appeal fell on deaf ears. We set off low in fuel.

I must explain here that in a carrier, as long as the twin exhausts are running, the water will not enter the twin ports in the rear sub-frame. Therefore it is possible to ford fairly deep water. The motor began to splutter as we forded the estuary until about halfway across it cut out due to the lack of fuel and we were swamped in about sixty seconds flat. The sea water surged inside and suddenly I realised I couldn't swim. The tide was running in at around five knots, debris floated from inside the carrier and we had to bale out fast. I yelled out at two natives fishing nearby in a small boat or canoe who reluctantly picked us up only after I flashed a revolver in their direction. The situation was desperate, but we reached the north bank safely.

I was fed and bedded for the night by the Punjabs. Their British officers welcomed me as an equal and I deeply appreciated the VIP treatment I received from their staff. I was very concerned for the carrier, but all attempts to salvage it were in vain and next morning all I could see above the water line was the Bren mounting rod tilted at about thirty degrees. She was sinking in the quicksands; gone forever. I felt sad at my misfortune, but my new-found friends treated me with great kindness and sent a horse-mounted DR back to base to inform my CO of my whereabouts.

### Christmas — 1942:

My arrival at the 5/8th Battalion Punjab HQ must have been towards the late afternoon of Christmas Day 1942. I had lost the carrier while others had been celebrating the coming of Christ and I found me a refuge among unexpected friends. The unit had a troop of beautiful chestnut horses, no doubt a well-known Punjabi breed, which were groomed with loving care by their handlers. Not many horses were to be found in forward areas and were more related with ceremonial parades. I admired the display of horsemanship by men obviously born in the saddle figuratively speaking, but sadly accidents can happen. The battalion defence perimeter was protected by three-tier coils of Dannet barbed wire concealed among the scrub and tall grass.

Early one morning about the 27th December, the colonel's groom was

35

exercising three horses while riding the middle one and leading the other two, one either side. Suddenly the high-spirited animals galloped into a fast canter, momentarily out of control. The colonel's mount charged straight into the concealed wire throwing the rider: the other two horses shied clear. The groom suffered multiple injuries and the horse was lacerated so badly it had to be shot. The groom may have died, but I am not quite sure. It was a tragic day for all concerned and I silently shared the grief of my new-found comrades as I left to join my unit, which was now in an area a few miles south of Maungdaw.

On returning to Maungdaw I was interviewed by an officer from brigade headquarters. He said they had already received the RE major's report, which stated that there were no Japanese troops between Maungdaw and Foul Point, and I was asked if I agreed with his observations. I told the officer that I honestly thought the major could be wrong and that we were being watched from the foothills, which is why I refused to drive back with headlights on. The cooking pots on the fire were further proof. I also stated that there was one solitary shot from the Donbaik direction in reply to our burst of fire from the Bren gun. My remarks were duly noted. The officer was inclined to agree with my report and said we should advance prepared for any possible contingency. This statement was not made on hindsight and my concern was well founded and confirmed later when we met the Japs on the beach just south of Indin, halfway down the Peninsula when the Punjabi Havildar (sergeant) Parkash Singh, was recommended for the VC. I remarked to my troop commander as we watched the event, "That man deserves the VC," and he agreed. It was now the end of another year.

### Action Stations — 1st January, 1943:

The brigade was ordered to advance south on a front covering the area between a long range of hills on the eastern flank, and a coastal strip approximately half a mile wide, fringed with a continuous sandy beach suitable for vehicular traffic. A dry-weather dirt road through scrub and paddy fields would follow later. The other side of the range of hills sloped towards the Kalapanzin river, which flowed south and west towards Foul Point at the tip of the Arakan-Mayu Peninsula. The Kaladan sector was approached by way of the Maungdaw and Buthidaung tunnels from the north — a once-planned rail route which would connect with Cox's Bazaar and Dohazari further north. Meanwhile another brigade would cover the eastern tunnel area while we were to proceed down the coast to Foul Point and consolidate.

My battery commander shared my suspicions concerning the possibility of Japs ahead and we advanced warily with infantry sweeping inland towards the foothills. A Punjabi carrier platoon of four vehicles kept ahead of our guns as we approached along the beach. Our column consisted of vehicles related to an eight-gun battery moving at intervals stretched out over a mile back.

Everything was quiet and deserted looking. Suddenly there was an erratic burst of gunfire and the leading carrier was knocked out about 500 yards ahead of us. The other three carriers fanned out as a group of Jap soldiers rushed out to seize their prize, but the carrier crews returned their fire forcing the enemy to run for cover. Meanwhile it was action stations as the leading guns were brought forward, muzzles pointed ahead across the open beach and loaded at the double. A shimmering heat haze blurred our vision as we looked towards the scene ahead. Orders were barked out, "Fire." The first shells landed as planned just ahead of the target then the range was carefully dropped to give the carrier platoon covering fire while a lone havildar (sergeant) rushed forward and rescued his wounded officer from the disabled leading carrier. As the platoon withdrew from the skirmish, our guns swept the area between the abandoned vehicle and the immediate sand dunes where enemy soldiers could be seen running back and forth in a state of frenzy. When the smoke cleared we pulled the guns off the beach and dug gun pits among the dunes, forming a defence perimeter in case of a counterattack.

Meanwhile the havildar's name went forward as a nomination for the Victoria Cross, and I reckoned he had earned it, apart from the fact that we had been mates together during my stay with the Punjabis at Alethangyaw. He taught me a few words in Hindi and shared his chapattis and curried chicken, cooked over a primitive-style fire. Most of the Punjabis did their own cooking, usually shared by groups of four. The basic flour, etc. was an issue, but a lot of foraging went on around the villages for chickens and vegetables. Beef and pork were taboo and goat flesh was about the only alternative meat available, whereas British troops relied on tinned corned beef and hard, very plain biscuits as our staple diet. There was not much else while in the forward areas. On the other hand, we would eat anything put in front of us when we were hungry — and that was all the time.

### Aerobatics — 2nd January, 1943:

When I left Maungdaw to rejoin my battery, I followed my original trail which was being formed into a dry-season road by a squad of Engineers. One nullah (creek) was bridged with a bamboo platform, perhaps strong enough for foot traffic, but when the first vehicle drove on to it, the bridge gently sunk into the shallow creek taking the truck with it. Happily there was no further damage and the gap was temporarily filled in. I arrived at the rendezvous and found my unit congregated alongside a large group of men and vehicles. The brigade was not too well camouflaged as another move was imminent.

As we awaited our instructions from an HQ conference being held nearby, a lone aircraft slowly drifted across the sky between the foothills and Maungdaw to the north, and continued west towards Alethangyaw on the coast. No one paid much attention at first, then we noticed that the pilot was concentrating more on us and started to bank and circle in a fascinating display of aerobatics. The plane was brightly painted red and gold with geometric designs as seen on planes at an air pageant. We started to wave at him and I believe he acknowledged as he banked once more before flying off. Yes, we did see the red spots on his wings, eventually! We could have brought him down with a Bren gun as he drifted slowly at a very low altitude. That pilot fooled the lot of us and deserved to get away for pure audacity, but sadly he must have returned to Jap HQ with some good pictures of our troop strength and movements. An unforgivable mistake on our part.

During my absence from Maungdaw while on reconnaissance to Foul Point my own carrier named RF was badly needing an overhaul as it had taken a hammering during our arduous journey round Elephant Point when the gun tractors sank in the quicksands and had to be rescued by unloading, digging out, winching, and manhandling with drag ropes, while the two carriers were used as anchors and bulldozers. I was at the helm in my vehicle for thirty-six hours. I fell asleep several times but the gunners kept waking me up with food and mugs of tea. We were fighting for our lives to save our precious equipment. We all did our whack for King and country, most of us on two bob per day and no overtime rates. The incoming tides were our biggest enemy.

Nothing was done to RF while the battery rested over Christmas. Some of our junior officers had played around with the carrier while I was absent, and on my return I found that due to their ignorance the vehicle defects had been multiplied. The clutch had needed attention, now I found a burnt-out clutch, the steering was stuffed and it was using gallons of water and oil. It also had badly worn gear selectors, possibly bent and I could only use first and reverse gears by holding the lever in position with my left foot across the gate. There had been no maintenance or routine checks for water and oil etc., and the bogie-wheel assemblies were without grease.

## Observation Post — 3rd January, 1943:

After a hurried conference at the command post, the OP personnel from E and F Troops were mustered in preparation for an expedition destined for the higher hills on our left flank forward of the gun positions.

There was to be an eight-gun full-battery barrage, therefore it had been decided to take double the usual required staff. Included in the group was the old man himself, Major William Breckinbridge. Theirs is not to reason why, but I failed to comprehend the size of the party (as it was often called) and was further puzzled by the amount of equipment we had to hump on our backs as well as a rifle and a bandolier of fifty rounds of

.303 ammunition. The equipment included a No. 11 wireless, normally used in a carrier or wireless truck. The set required two very heavy 6V accumulators, aerial and ancillary equipment, i.e. mike, headphones, ground-aerial leads and remote-control phone unit. We also had a signalling lamp, field telephone, heliograph and tripod, steel helmet and a blanket each as we may stay away for some time, rations of sorts and water bottles. Pack mules were unsuitable where we were to go.

The party moved off early. It was January 3rd, 1943. We crossed a tidal estuary a short distance ahead of the guns then we turned left and moved straight ahead towards the same creek further inland. The water was chest high as we waded across, carrying our delicate instruments above our heads then returning for the remainder. The hot sun began to beat down on us as we wallowed under our load and approached the bamboo-clad slopes ahead, rising straight up, pointing to a cloudless sky. The climb began immediately as we slithered on the wet, slimy undergrowth, the base of the bamboo stems giving us the only foothold. The men cursed their dilemma and I wondered how we would ever make it, but we did eventually and the summit offered us a welcome respite. Nothing but thick bamboo-covered valleys and scrub could be seen, except the distant dunes and ocean behind us to the west.

The signallers tuned in the wireless, but due to excess static it was declared useless. However, the field telephone was working OK hooked on a single-line earth-return circuit. Later in the afternoon we called up the guns to send over a few single ranging shots. The ranges were confirmed and plotted on a sketched chart, and as the trajectory required a high angle of sight we used a charge-two cartridge so that the guns had to fire at a higher elevation. This was the chief characteristic of a howitzer compared with a field gun, which used a fixed shell-cartridge combination similar in design to a rifle bullet. We closed down for the night but maintained a listening watch.

Next morning, 4th January, the stage was set for the impending barrage, which duly arrived on schedule much closer than predicted. All hell was let loose. We were not dug in, the peak of the hill was rock hard, we were in the direct line of fire and it soon became obvious that the trajectory was too low. Too late — shells were bursting all around us. It quickly dawned on me that the guns were firing on charge three instead of charge two as directed the night before, for I had sent the message but it had subsequently been converted down at the command post in error. Screaming shells were exploding everywhere. I threw myself hard against a fallen tree and could hardly believe it was our own guns. The shells were classed as anti-personnel, which meant they explode virtually on touching the mere surface causing the maximum surface concussion as well as the shrapnel from the metal casing itself. Soon there were the inevitable screams from wounded comrades suffering from terrible wounds and calling for help. I

39

could feel my body being violently compressed with every explosion. The pungent smell of cordite was everywhere while shrapnel whined all around us.

## *Observation Post — 4th January, 1943:*

'Angry shells' was a term used by old soldiers when one happened to be at the receiving end, and my experience could never have been more fittingly described. Due to the accuracy and concentration inadvertently brought down on us by our own gunners, it was sheer hell let loose on unsuspecting victims.

Just as suddenly and on a predicted pattern, I jumped up as the barrage ceased temporarily. I knew there would be a ten-minute interval as I clambered back to my post. The wireless and phone were out of action, but the heliograph was miraculously still intact. Racing against time before the next onslaught, I turned to my BC who was calm though mortally wounded while our troop captain nursed a wrist wound and Lieutenant Cornelius attended the dismembered and dying. "OK to order a cease fire, sir?"

"Yes, Signaller, do what you can, don't mind me." Then he added "Give him some whisky out of my haversack will you, Cornelius. Someone must get a message through to the guns. Carry on, Signaller!"

Bob Picken appeared from nowhere, dazed but still in one piece, and a second signaller joined us as we set up the heliograph. I tried to pinpoint the gun position when a second barrage opened up in a more concentrated fury. The hellish carnage was repeating itself as my wounded mates received further punishment. I could tell by heart-rending renewed cries for help. If animals had to suffer such agonies it would be classed as humane to terminate their hopeless situation, I was in an unenviable position and had to refuse them an act of mercy.

I waited for the next lull, rushed up to assess the damage and discovered Picken was missing while my other signaller lay stiff beside a scorched blanket at the nearest shell's point of impact, a mere dent on the ground surface. My friend was peppered with small pieces of shrapnel; his death had been instantaneous. I searched around and found the heliograph still intact, but the hinged legs of the tripod a bit wobbly.

I wasted no time and flashed SOS continuously towards the shimmering sand dunes. Lieutenant Cornelius handed me a second cup of Old Angus whisky then offered to write the message as I sent and received the Morse signals. We had no message pad but used my AB64 army pay book instead. I continued to send SOS hoping it would be seen by someone, bearing in mind that a heliograph beam has only an eight foot beam dispersal over one mile, gradually widening according to distance. It was a trying experience. My dying comrades were calling me by name to help them, but there was nothing we could do except get a first-aid team to fetch morphine and shovels.

Time dragged on as I relentlessly tried to pinpoint the gun-position signallers. I had a persistent nature and it paid off when a flicker of light beamed on me slightly to my left. I focused my mirrors on the new location, repeated SOS twice then sent a short message for immediate assistance using G-for-George procedure, where every letter was sent twice. This method was to prevent the enemy from picking up the flashes from the other station which faced the enemy territory. There was a long pause. All I required was a long dash for acknowledgement, but instead they signalled me 'in clear' asking me who I was and where did I live. It was obvious they were puzzled; perhaps they thought it was an enemy hoax. I replied in our local doric vernacular spelling, which seemed to convince them.

Lieutenant Cornelius wrote down the answer we'd hoped and prayed for: "Aldridge and stretcher-bearers leaving immediately. How many casualties?" That was the memorial written inside the back pages of my now long-lost army pay book.

The rescue team climbed those soul-destroying, greasy bamboo slopes in record time. I had held on as long as I could and was very deep in shock. My past youthful life surged through my brain and for a fleeting moment I had a clear vision of my dear mother. Although I was not religious, she always took us to church on Sundays but, for no reason I can think of, the old hymn 'Rock of Ages' softly came to my mind. It was the turning point in my fight for mental survival. My mother brought me into this world and it was for her that I had to fight on. Sentimental, you may think, but we all need an anchor in life and she was mine.

My body was in a state of collapse, but I felt I had done my duty for my helpless, dying comrades whom I shall always remember. I write hoping their deaths have not been in vain.

As the stretcher party arrived after an arduous climb through bamboo-covered mud and scrub, the medical orderly administered morphine to my mortally wounded comrades, whose weakening and relentless cries for help had added further to my own horrifying experience — especially as my name was repeatedly raised in their anguished appeals for help. Their wounds were so hopeless that it was futile to move them.

I was duly ordered back to the gun position and told to report to the RAP first-aid tent as I was very weak and in deep shock. The second measure of whisky was having a numbing effect on my troubled brain, but I was confident that I could make the return journey alone. On that assurance I was allowed to leave the OP.

I wore the troop commander's web harness which contained his compass, .38 ammo, his revolver in its web holster and binoculars. Furthermore, I carried my Lee-Enfield .303 rifle and a cloth bandolier with fifty rounds draped loosely over my shoulder. I set off hoping to find the broken telephone line and follow it back to the gun position.

Soon after leaving the OP I found a faint track among the scrub and followed it. I stumbled along for about half an hour until I became so weak that my legs crumpled by the side of the track. I must have passed out. The sun was almost straight above so it would be about noon. I remembered all that much later when I awoke to see the sun heading west about 4 p.m.

Gradually my head cleared. I stood up and took my bearings, finding myself in enemy territory as I had been travelling south instead of west! I quickly realised that I should retrace my steps and find a burn (stream) which would take me to the beach — a thought that failed to occur to me earlier. I suddenly became aware of my plight and took desperate steps to get moving again in spite of my weakness.

I committed an unforgivable crime by removing the bolt in my rifle, throwing it uphill and well off the track, then doing likewise with the rifle in the opposite direction: that is as far downhill into the deep scrub as gravity allowed it to travel. About fifty yards further on, I swung the cloth bandolier far and wide into impenetrable bamboo bush. My burden was no longer hindering my progress and I was still armed with the revolver and compass.

I found a small stream and traced it down a steep V-shaped gully. I was on my way at last. I waded and clung to clefted fissures in the rugged miniature ravine until it finally widened sufficiently to allow a broken but watery shingle pathway, gradually levelling out towards the dunes far below. As I slid and fell on my way down, I rounded a blind bend among the shingle and boulders and stumbled head on into a Gurkha patrol, very much at the ready.

I stopped dead on the track and faced about a dozen stern-faced men, literally armed to the teeth. Thank goodness my face was an ashen white, illuminated with fear and could not be mistaken for a Mongol-faced Jap. The white officer came forward in amazement and asked where I had come from. I explained the best I could. He remarked how lucky I was not to get shot, and wished me luck on my way down, adding that I didn't look well either. He was right there as I was semi-delirious with fatigue and weak with hunger as I had no food since early morning apart from a few biscuits with sweetened condensed milk washed down with a mouthful of water from my flask.

As the going got easier I gained confidence and hoped to reach my parked Bren carrier before nightfall as there was virtually no twilight in that part of the world. Suddenly there were loose stones and debris rumbling down from my right and as I stood in suspense, two stretcher-bearers emerged. They were Punjabis carrying a dead comrade all the way back to the beach, to be ultimately cremated in a funeral pyre made with rocks and driftwood. The deceased soldier had been attached to our ill-fated OP as an observer in liaison with our unit. I stood in solemn silence as he passed towards his ultimate destination.

I reached the Bren carrier standing derelict on the sand dunes on the south side of the tidal estuary. The gun positions were out of sight beyond the northern bank. I was very much alone and had to cross the incoming tidal creek regardless and unaided! The snag was that I couldn't swim, but neither could I wait a further twelve hours or so until the next low tide. I was still carrying the revolver, etc. which would weigh me down, but I was desperate to cross that creek so I unharnessed myself and placed the troop commander's equipment in the Bren carrier. Then I waded into the water, ultimately finding myself scared but afloat in a vertical posture. I bounced my feet on the sandy bottom and kicked myself gradually across the incoming tide, finally touching the bottom with both feet some hundred yards upstream, where I waded ashore. I eventually found the command post where I was greeted in almost total silence. We all mourned our dead comrades now being buried on Conical Hill as they passed away mercifully one by one.

My morale was shattered. I felt like a lost dog, broken in spirit and not knowing which way to turn. It soon became obvious that it would take years to suppress my shell-shocked state of mind and live down the recurring nightmares. No one could be expected to fully understand such a situation unless they had been through a similar experience and were able to regain a reasonable and rational state of sanity.

The sceptics use words like exaggerations, cowards and yellow while others call the victim a liar only to perhaps find later that they are more likely to have been reflecting their own inner imperfections.

On that fateful day one thing was proved to me regardless of uninitiated critics: which is, a shell could burst and within a six-foot radius one man could be peppered with shrapnel, another blown out of sight dazed but physically unharmed, while a third person could be violently compressed and also physically unharmed. This is what happened to three signallers while in the process of sending signals using Morse on a heliograph standing on open ground. Why three men? One reads the distant signal, the second writes it down and the third trims the mirrors to the ever-moving sunlight as he stands by to transmit while always tuned to the other station.

We were subjected to eight 25-pounder guns each firing rapidly on a fixed target for ten solid minutes followed by a pause of ten minutes: a sequence which was repeated until they were ordered to cease fire. We accidentally happened to be the target and hence the reason for my involvement. It could be likened to being inside an eight-cylinder combustion engine and having the living daylight pummelled out of you coupled with the noise and stench of cordite. Add the screams and cries for help from ghastly wounded and dying personal friends and some picture should emerge.

But please don't call that person a liar. Nor does he want sympathy. Just let him feel secure among his fellow comrades — that is all the help he requires. The rest is up to him.

### *The Resurrection:*

Before going into hospital, having just returned from the OP suffering from shell-shock, the BSM told me to check the Bren carrier as we were to take part in an attack along with a few Valentine tanks in an attempt to push the enemy out of the area around Donbaik. I discovered that the carrier had been mishandled by an unauthorised person — the engine had a cracked block and worn gear selectors, and the steering was stuffed, requiring a thirty-six foot turning circle. I reported the situation to the BSM, also adding that I was unfit to drive it in any case. I was a physical and mental wreck. My legs wanted to crumble under me and the sound of a motorbike starting was enough to make me shake with uncontrollable fear. The BSM blew up with rage and said I was yellow, and I retorted by asking him to test it himself. He knew how to drive the carrier but he refused and later ordered a quad driver to take over.

The MO had wanted me to go into hospital a few days earlier when I first arrived back from the OP, but I thought I would come right with a bit of rest and feeling safe among my comrades. The rest was not to be, so I reported to his RP tent. All he said was, "I wondered when you would turn up," I left in the next ambulance.

I later learned that the carrier packed up a few hundred yards from base and had to be abandoned, much to the relief of the driver and other occupants. The Valentines found the terrain unsuitable to manoeuvre and the attack was abandoned. I saw the tanks parked about eighty miles north at Cox's Bazaar when I was returning to the front line weeks later.

While I was in hospital, the Japs encircled some of our troops immediately north of Donbaik. Bob Picken was one of them; he was unaccounted for and was subsequently reported 'missing presumed killed'. I was duly informed but I was not convinced that he was dead. I deliberately checked every man I could find who escaped and knew Bob, but no one saw him fall. The only glimmer of hope came when one lad said he last saw him making for the hills. On that statement I pinned my hopes and prayed he was still alive with a slim chance he had been taken prisoner. However, the official citation was conveyed to his mother and family and I soldiered on, alone, like a twin who had lost the other half of himself. One officer asked me to write a letter sending our condolences to his family, which I reluctantly did. I didn't write to his mother, who was grief-stricken, but to his brother who worked and lived in the neighbouring town of Prestwick, Ayrshire. I warned him to secrecy that it was still my belief that Bob might have been taken prisoner. I knew I was sticking my neck out, but that was my sole reason for writing in the first place! The bond between us persisted. I never gave up hope and I shouldered an extra burden keeping my thoughts on the matter very much to myself. I soldiered on detesting war more than ever but never gave up hope.

It couldn't last forever. I was to survive a few near misses until I was sent back to Deolali prior to repatriation. Bob was missing from January 1943 to July/August 1945 (two and a half years). Then one day the postman casually handed me a letter in a vaguely familiar handwriting postmarked Delhi. Bob had returned from the dead. I was quite surprised in a way. It hadn't dawned on me that he might just want to write to me first giving a few details relating to his absence.

He was captured in the foothills north of Donbaik. He explained to his captors that he was only an errand boy who knew nothing, and acted dumb and stupid. They sent him to Rangoon where he was treated as a coolie, unloading sampans, and because he was a barber he had to cut the Japanese commander's hair. He wore only a dhoti, had his head shaved and no footwear, his feet developed thick calloused skin which had to be rehabilitated over a period of three weeks during his stay recuperating in Delhi before he could once more wear a pair of shoes. Eventually he and his fellow ex-prisoners got the chance to fly home. They made a forced landing in the Persian Gulf area, were rescued, and taken to Bahrain I think. Those who had had enough adventure were given the option to proceed home by boat, but our friend, Bob, decided it was all the way for him, whereby he finally made it!

His 'resurrection' was duly celebrated in my absence back home in Kilmarnock. It was sometime before I finally caught up with him. We were both a bit thinner and older looking. We had lost our boyish features and had suddenly emerged back to a hard and cold war-torn world. The people at home had suffered too, some more than others. We had all made sacrifices, many didn't make it. We were the lucky ones.

Bob Picken earned his immediate discharge as an ex-prisoner of war, and now makes his own way in the world, enjoying reasonable success and is now chairman of the local Regional Co-op Society. We still correspond across the hemispheres hoping to meet again in the near future, and relive the lighter moments of yesteryear.

Since writing this story, it has come to hand that our friend, Bob, was forced to serve six months in solitary confinement while a POW in Rangoon. During this time he was interrogated every ten days, and in order to keep fit, he manipulated his limbs in a very confined space when the Japanese guards were not around to restrain him. When finally they escaped, they met up with British troops in Pegu from where they were flown to Comilla in Bengal. There they were visited by General Bill Slim and stage star Paula Green and were treated like VIPs.

They were all told that when they got back to Britain, because of their hideous ordeal, they would never need to work again and every one of them should have enough money to live in comfort and travel the world. Bob tells me that is why he joined the Post Office! At least that is what his boss told him!

Honest Bob we call him — you either love him or hate his guts — he hasn't changed a bit. God bless him and men like him. As with his enthusiasm for table tennis, he plays to win.

## Arakan — Night Manoeuvre — 1943:

The guns were in position on the sand dunes just up off the beach, and when the crews took their turn at having a dip in the rolling surf, bathing suits were an optional extra! On the call 'Action Stations!' it was an amusing sight to see every mother's son race to his post, dressed as God intended, the gunlayer sitting on the hot seat already anticipating the orders from the command post, which was in constant communication with the forward observation post, normally manned by at least one officer, a specialist assistant and two signallers. The whole operation depended on teamwork; every man could therefore proudly claim to be a gunner of the Royal Artillery. Hence I was called gunner/signaller, a necessary member of the team. No time was wasted getting those shells into the air, in a way, the gunners enjoyed their work if only because they thought that what they were doing was necessary.

On one occasion, a few Japanese bombers were returning south and so happened to jettison their load, more by chance than judgement, on our camouflaged positions, thereby exposing all below them while cartridge cases and bags of cordite flared up in all directions. It was a miniature holocaust. Men were buried alive in their slit trenches and there was confusion for a short while. The BSM took off to the foothills and had to be escorted back to the gun positions. He once yelled to me that I was yellow when badly shell-shocked.

It was obvious that the site would be plotted for further attention by the Japs and the battery commander was quick to realise what the outcome would be. A new gun position was reconnoitred and plans drawn up before the evening sun slipped over the Bay of Bengal. That night the battery moved under the cover of darkness, leaving a carelessly camouflaged gun position intact. Tracks made during the night were carefully wiped from the direction of our new positions. The stage was set. Our visitors returned next morning with reinforcements and circled their target. In all fairness, the Japs did a good job, leaving craters all over the place. Nothing was left that could be termed recoverable. We forgot to leave a forwarding address!

One lad was sent to hospital who had been burned, buried alive and was suffering from an advanced state of shock. I hope he got over his ordeal as I lost touch with him. He was a good comrade and a first class signaller. I think he came from Chorley, Lancashire. Many of our lads did, as well as a few from Yorkshire. They joined us at Selkirk in the early days of the war, and fitted in well with their Scottish counterparts, but they were disappointed to find that we didn't wear kilts! However, we had a good pipe band, which volunteered as a band in 1939. Most of the bandsmen came from Irvine and Saltcoats in Ayrshire.

### Arakan Surprise Attack — 1943:

Having rejoined the battery after a spell in hospital, I was told to remain at the gun position and make myself useful, which I did by taking my turn on the No. 11 wireless using W/T (Morse only), and situated by the command post dugout.

During my rest up top I slept under a bush. On one occasion, it was during early morning darkness, the sound of the guns firing intermittently lulled us to sleep and the gentle heaving of the ground shock waves added to the depth of our slumbers as we were exhausted after long spells of static and code signals crashing in the headphones.

During that particular night I dreamt of something moving at a snail's pace across my chest, but I was so tired that I couldn't force myself to wake up properly. However, when I eventually did, it was terrifying. My hair bristled with fright, my heart almost stopped beating and I willed myself not to breathe — which was utterly impossible of course! But slowly, inch — pause — inch — pause — inch at a time, my nightmare finally trailed itself beyond my rigid body. I must have collapsed with fear and exhaustion. When I reawoke, my mate gave me a mug of tea then I slipped into the dugout and donned the headphones once more, having told my mate about my dream. A short time later, it was now daylight, my mate yelled out, "Come and see this!" There stretched out across the branches of the bush was the transparent skin shed by a snake about three-foot long! No further comment from me . . .

About that time, something unusual was happening far behind us. We could hear shooting going on and then we heard that Brigade HQ had been attacked! Apparently a large group of Japs, stated to be Imperial Guards, had swept down from the hills and virtually massacred our more or less unguarded HQ staff. Our brigadier was captured and the Japs announced later that he died of wounds.

While we were virtually cut off between the hills and the sea, troops were rushed back to drive the attackers off, but were only partially successful. We had to try and save the guns so steps were immediately implemented to evacuate our positions. A slim chance lay along the beach. We withdrew to the sand dunes almost in line with what was once Brigade HQ, where we stood to all through the night — that is, all except yours truly. I was running a temperature of 105° due to malaria and my left leg was swollen due to a gash in the calf muscle. The orderly painted my leg with something and the

47

battery sergeant major made me lie down and drink a pint mug of rum!

I slept well that night, then at dawn next morning we got ready for the break-out. Every vehicle not required was immobilised and abandoned because we had only enough petrol left to get the remainder back to safety. It was now or never. Each vehicle in turn ran the gauntlet across the open paddy and onto the beach proper. We all made it, I think.

On drawing opposite Brigade HQ the gunners dropped their trails (gun) and, over open sights, blasted away at the enemy. When HE ran out, they continued firing using smoke and armour-piercing shells which were now surplus baggage anyway! The Japs replied with captured three-inch mortars, but forgot to set the fuses! Lucky for us, as they were right on target! During this action, our sister battery, the 316th, came up and covered our withdrawal by setting up a smokescreen. This distracted the Japs and we finally broke through to our own lines.

We later learned that a gun blew up (premature) and some of the crew (316th) were killed. That battery was commanded by Major 'Bill' Breckinbridge, cousin to our late BC who was killed earlier. We had a mutual respect for each other.

Our unit had to withdraw further back to re-form and, while doing so, had to run the gauntlet once again as a Jap long-range machine-gun was covering our route inland from the beach. I was driving a truck some distance behind E Troop's, carrier, when it pulled up ahead. Someone had fallen off so the crew baled out, picked up their comrade, and took off again. As we moved on again, there were two thuds into the right mudguard of my cab. I lifted my foot off the throttle and I saw two holes in the metal immediately below the sole of my right foot! We turned off once more towards the beach about a mile further on, just in time to see the carrier crew lay our fallen comrade to the ground. He was dead with a bullet through his head. Another signaller was laid to rest on a foreign strand. I still remember his tin hat hanging on a branch above his grave. A few weeks earlier, his wife had asked him for a divorce as she wanted to marry a Yank. It broke his heart, but his death was a fluke — she got her divorce.

We reached a khal which held us up for a while until the tide receded, then one by one we winched the vehicles across, dried out the motors, and moved on towards Maungdaw. The fever caught up with me and I was finally bundled off to hospital; my left leg was swollen and festering.

It was then I boarded the *Wusueh* hospital ship for Calcutta (Loretto Convent). As I was delirious at times, my memory is vague, but I do remember the ship very clearly. It had a Chinese crew and British officers and nursing staff. To us it was a cruise ship — everything was spotless and civilised. Before we boarded the ship I met our Regimental Sergeant Major Hill. He was the smartest soldier I ever met and a credit to the British Army. He earned the respect of all who served under him. He was the Father of the Regiment when it was first formed in 1939.

The *Wusueh* was warned by the Jap radio to stop carrying arms and ammunition on its return trips or it would be sunk! The British hotly denied the accusations, but it was a possibility nevertheless! That was for Intelligence to sort out.

I once travelled to hospital from Chittagong to Calcutta on a British freighter of about 9,000 tons. It was clean and had a small crew and it may have had Red Cross sheets tied across the decks or bulkheads.

## Arakan Hospital — 1943:

My journeys to hospital were determined by the very nature of the environment we had to endure over long periods of privation, malnutrition, and lack of sleep. The pace was relentless, frustrating and soul destroying. We were trapped in a vacuum and the situation was stalemate. Morale was low and the operation was bogged down by the obvious lack of communication between HQ in Delhi and the far and very remote front line. The line was held by the Inniskilling Fusiliers who were forever under attack from the well dug-in enemy among the surrounding foothills. Their casualties were constantly high and I can remember when they were receiving around ninety replacements nightly, as they could only move forward under the cover of darkness. The wounded had to lie out all through the day waiting for nightfall before receiving medical attention. Vultures were for ever soaring above the battle area.

We all had a very low blood count, consequently any disease floating around was contracted by the victim whether he was large or small. In fact, the short, wiry bloke recovered more quickly than his larger counterpart. One elderly doctor in Loretto Convent Hospital noticed that all his patients kept coming in a continuous stream, always from the same units. He told us we were all suffering from malnutrition and what is now called battle fatigue. Off his own bat he put us all on special rations (fresh food) and three weeks' convalescence. Our physical health was rapidly improved and our morale improved simultaneously. Sheets and pyjamas were a great luxury and a bath was the ultimate in our memories of hospital comforts.

My first visit to Loretto Convent was with shell-shock and the journey was a long drawn-out affair by road, rail, river boat and finally hospital train to Calcutta. I will always remember the padre who tried to inveigle me into believing that my illness could only be cured by adopting his philosophy, otherwise I would have a curse on me for the rest of my life! I was invited to his house within the grounds of the convent on the pretext of just afternoon tea and a chat about the outside world. His batman served tea in the study. The tray had cigarettes, a selection of cakes and then he walked in, apologising for being late. We talked about my family, school and my hobbies. I was there a fair while, then I got up to leave thanking him for his hospitality, when suddenly he changed his serene composed manner and firmly pushed a Bible into my hand saying, "There is no hope for you unless you accept my spiritual guidance, and this Bible is the key to your salvation!"

I smiled at him for it was apparent it had been a battle of wits and his ruse had failed. I returned his Bible by laying it on the table and told him not to insult my intelligence as I would get over this shell-shock regardless of his predictions. It took many years and nightmares but the ultimate faith is in oneself. The padre cunningly bypassed my bed every day from then on. I finally discharged myself as I wanted to get back to my mates and collect my home mail.

My second visit to Loretto Convent was with malaria and a badly inflamed calf muscle on the left leg, which I had procured while encircled during the capture and annihilation of our Brigade HQ. The wound was six inches long and half an inch wide with a deep V-shaped groove. Green and yellow pus suppurated from the open flesh. The malaria took its usual course and left me weak but undaunted. I was determined to do something about my leg. The medical heads talked about a gunshot wound and amputation, but I thought otherwise! As the treatment seemed inadequate, I got out of bed and dragged myself along to the top of the ward to have a word with the male orderly who dispensed the treatment. He was an old soldier and I asked if he had any sulphanilamide paste. He knew what I meant, pointed to a large jar in the cabinet stating that it was more than his job was worth to give it to me, but laid out some white lint and bandages on a table and turned away! I proceeded to spread the paste on like butter, covering the lint which was eight inches by four. I was on the point of slapping it on the pus-infested wound when in walked the ward sister. She went into a rage but I held my ground. Defiantly I finished dressing the wound and dragged myself back along the ward and into bed.

Next morning my leg felt cool and comfortable for the first time in many weeks. The MO and matron duly came round the ward with sister at the rear! No comment so far. When the dressing was removed there was no pus; the wound was dry and the flesh was a pale, healthy pink. Slowly smiles appeared on the onlookers' faces and a tear rolled down the dear matron's cheek. Sister remained silent. "Carry on with the same treatment, Sister!" The MO was pleased with my sudden progress! I still have the scar to prove it.

When I finally left Loretto, the sister handed me a jar of paste and half a dozen bandages. She also wished me best of luck and told me to take care of myself as I was still only a boy with an innocent baby face. I was just turned twenty-two!

I will always remember a military band playing the 'Barcarole' in the grounds of the convent, highlighted by the trumpet solo emerging from the shrubbery as the notes gradually became louder. It was a memorable occasion — that tune still haunts me.

Sulphanilamide was made known to me by our medical orderly, who crushed M and B tablets into powder and mixed them with petroleum jelly to treat septic jungle sores. Patent ointments became neutralised by sweat, and were therefore useless under tropical conditions.

Once, when in Calcutta on leave, I got a bad tummyache and was taken to a first-aid post where I had the honour to meet Lady and Sir Ameer Ali (chief justice of Calcutta High Court). They made me their guest and I was treated by their private physician and experienced the truly wonderful hospitality of highly respected but humble members of the old world aristocracy. Lady Ameer also helped to run a soup kitchen for the thousands of destitute inhabitants of Calcutta. Many had drifted in from outlying districts to swell their numbers as there was a famine sweeping the eastern area of India. This had been brought about by the tillers of the soil deserting their paddy fields to earn a few rupees working for military installations, such as coolie labour for roads and airstrips.

Many died on the streets or alleyways and children (infants) lay beside their dead mothers in the European area of Chowringhee. I saw children foraging for food among the garbage cans left out in the streets, while stray dogs were kept at bay. I once called in to the WVS centre in Dalhousie Square, telephoned the city council and told them there were at least a dozen bodies lying out on the street between Chowringhee and Dalhousie Square. I was told that it was uneconomical to send a truck out for less than twenty! Sir Ameer Ali got in touch with central government in Delhi and asked for assistance. They contacted the Punjab State government who replied that grain was available, but they would require the cash in advance! Sir Ameer bought a lot from his own private account, worth thousands of rupees, and collected more from friends and associates around Calcutta. The food centre had to be kept going. This was a 'normal' famine — the hierarchy were not unduly concerned, so it was left to a few to bear the moral obligations of a corrupt society. India was run on graft; those who were at the bottom of the social ladder fell and died by the wayside.

I got to understand the local language and could converse with the native communities around Bengal. They told me I spoke bazaar Hindustani and could throw in a few Bengali words to the delight of the locals. One ack-ack artillery officer told me not to speak with the natives as we were members of the British Raj! I replied that they were human beings just the same as we were. I ignored his pompous remarks and hoped the ordinary wartime squaddies would continue to treat all Indians as equals.

We had no divine right to dominate and bully the subservient races or castes of any nation. Lord Louis Mountbatten had the right idea, furthermore they trusted and respected him. He rose above politics and handed over the reigns of government with dignity and respect, treating our Indian brothers of the Commonwealth with equality. Later was born Pakistan, then Bangladesh; they still had problems, but this time we can not blame the British, thank goodness!

One earlier visit to hospital was at Comilla where we ran out of quinine and only the severest cases could get treatment. I once held a kerosene lamp for the MO as he gave my mate in the next bed an intravenous injection as he was unable to swallow and hold down the quinine in the usual manner. Frank Caven was down from thirteen stone to a mere seven! He recovered. Later we managed to switch to mepacrine and eventually we got the tablets from our own MO and treated ourselves. It was no longer recognised by the army as a disease. All told I contracted malaria seven times!

### Comilla Station — 1943:

Large contingents of troops were moving across Bengal to Comilla then south to the Arakan. Many were returning from hospital or leave, while a third group were in transit as reinforcements to such units as the Inniskillings or the 6th Infantry Brigade. The Assam-Bengal Railway was the main means of transport and operated on a metre-gauge track system east of the mighty Brahmaputra Delta, using steam locomotives with a variety of wooden-seated carriages and the odd first class coach.

It was almost dusk as we attempted to scramble aboard the long troop train standing on a siding, belching steam from her smokestack, denoting that her departure was imminent. My travelling companion and I found the packed train difficult to board, as most of the personnel were crammed Indian fashion, i.e. bulging out the doors and windows. The whistle blew and my mate yelled "We'll never make it!"

Suddenly it occurred to me there was a first class compartment at the end of the train, which looked empty from where we were standing on the track. As the heavy train started to stretch the coaches forward, I yelled out "Come on, this'll do us, Jock." I jumped on the running board, flung the door open, threw my gear on the floor, then hauled my mate aboard the now moving train. We just made it.

It was only then that I came face to face with a brigadier-general, sitting alone in a comfortable corner of the upholstered compartment looking at us quizzically, half in surprise, and in two minds whether to order us off, or congratulate us for initiative! He appeared to choose the latter, fortunately for us. We were told to sit down and introduce ourselves. We had a long journey ahead of us before we would reach Dohazari, east of Chittagong, springboard to the Arakan Peninsula.

One wall of the square-shaped compartment was stacked high with wooden cases, some marked gin, and others whisky. Our host explained that he was acting quartermaster on this trip on behalf of his brother officers, somewhere down the line. A noble deed indeed. We found our host pleasant and most sincere; in fact, a proper gentleman. He was familiar with what was happening in this first Arakan campaign and mentioned a brother officer in the Royal Engineers who had fittingly been promoted to colonel in the field and recommended for the MC as a result of his exploits during a reconnaissance down to Foul Point in the early days of the campaign. The information intrigued me as the same officer recommended me for a court martial, accusing me of "deliberately ditching a Bren gun carrier". My battery commander tore up the charge after hearing my own version of the incident. However, I had no desire to involve the brigadier, but did add that I had been the driver on that momentous occasion. In reply he congratulated me for doing an equally fine job. I was deeply impressed with the kind gentleman's remarks. I often found that high-ranking officers invariably earned my respect. They tended to look upon others as fellow human beings, as no man enjoys being made to look inferior.

### Ranchi and Poona — 1943-44:
The battery was finally pulled out of the Arakan and I rejoined them en route to Ranchi where we were to regroup. The rail journey took us by way of Asansol, which was a coaling place for the railway engines. The tenders were loaded by hand by a relay of women coolies who walked a plank from the loading bank carrying baskets of coal on their heads more elegantly than any mannequin ever could. The temperature was around 130° Fahrenheit and we sweltered in the stifling heat just watching them!

Our lips cracked and noses bled with the dry, furnace-like heat and we lay with our feet out of the windows as the train once more got on the move, climbing through the seemingly endless, undulating arid desert towards Ranchi. When we finally got there it was not the oasis we had expected and we formed yet another camp of tents and marquees many miles from nowhere. The dust storms were numerous and whirlwinds spiralled in unpredictable directions lifting marquees like parachutes where the white ants had been at work among the knots pegged to the guy ropes.

I was in charge of the signal stores and slept in the stores marquee as guard and caretaker. Anything missing could not be written off as 'lost in action' unless proof could be established. The British Army had a regulation which stated that, 'you shall pay for the one you lost and the replacement'. We never lost much gear if it was at all avoidable. Non-magnetic wireless watches were requested by the odd senior NCO or WO, but I always got their signature. One such WO tried to swear he had returned his borrowed watch and accused me of pilfering it. I signed a sworn statement and handed it to the CO that the WO still had the watch. It was returned within the twenty-four hours' ultimatum given to the man concerned. One man sent to assist me went outside to tighten the guy ropes and started to play about with a funny kind of worm with a very short stick. On going to investigate, I pulled him away from the krait or snake, which was no more than eight inches long. I killed it with a shovel — he was lucky.

During my stay in Ranchi, I was in my charpoy having a rest in the afternoon when I must have fallen asleep. I woke up later to find the signal sergeant and a mate holding me gently as I was coming out of a nightmare. I felt as weak as a child. The shell-shock was still having an effect on my subconscious mind. I always felt safe when my mates were around and my biggest dread was that I might get posted away from them. If I was downgraded medically, could they keep me on the strength? I was told no, as they were to reform and become a combined operations unit in which every man had to be A1 plus!

I was later put before a medical panel of two doctors who downgraded me to B2, but I stayed with the unit for a while longer when they moved to Poona Cavalry Barracks. We were billeted in the stables as the barracks were used as a general hospital. The charpoys were infested with bugs and the CO got the cooks to boil huge urns of water so that the beds could be immersed one end at a time. Finally we left our beds outside for the wee birds to pick them clean in the strong sun.

From memory, we had Christmas 1943 and New Year 1944 at Poona during our spell out of the line. Some officers relaxed their aloofness and joined the boys in a friendly drink, sharing a cigarette or having a friendly chat as a mark of comradeship. This came about because of the hardships they had shared mutually in battle. However, this state of affairs could not be tolerated by the top brass and some good officers were posted to other units. One officer was awarded the MC on behalf of his men, while he himself was in hospital. The men didn't approve of his award and nearly created a riot. The officer concerned had to make a hasty retreat from the dining hall during the presentation. I hope he kept quiet about it in later years.

I made myself useful around camp at Poona and often drove the duty truck into town. Our trucks were run down and one quad was using oil heavily yet it had only 12,000 miles on the clock. The reason was obvious: we had to crawl and winch most of the way down the Arakan as proper roads were unheard of. My carrier used petrol at one mile per gallon as first gear was normal except on firm sand.

I once travelled down to Bombay as a courier and was invited by the European driver on the electric train to travel on the footplate. It was a very interesting experience and I also learned that an Indian driver was paid 200 rupees per month, a Eurasian was paid 400 rupees while the European received 600. The latter drove the best electric units and that meant no 'steamers'. The main line was all electric between Poona and Bombay.

While at Poona we were on a diet of soya links three times a day for weeks on end, until the lads told the CO we'd had more than our fair share. Neither the camp dogs nor the chicos would look at the infernal meatless sausages. There were about three tons still in stock in the QM stores. The CO asked for volunteers and during the hours of darkness we buried the lot! Fresh rations were procured from the surrounding markets and morale soared immediately. I heard no more word about Bob Picken, but I never gave up hope.

I was finally posted back east alone to Dohazari, springboard to the Arakan. This time it was to the ack-ack (Bofors) as a signaller once more. I was sent down to the Karnaphuli railway/road bridge where we had a few Bofors on either side of the river. Our HQ was on the Chittagong side and I was DR on numerous occasions, which meant I had to ride over the makeshift-roadway part of the high rail bridge, which had taken quite a few lives with trucks running off and dropping into the river far below. Drivers seemed to lose their nerve and swerve off the planked decking. Later on, the army rigged bamboo matting either side of the track to screen the murky brown water from distracting the drivers.

Months later a convoy passed our way, which I quickly identified as the 494 Battery, and standing in the front vehicle was my old troop commander, now BC and promoted to major, heading for Admin Box area, east and south of Cox's Bazaar. I felt a lump in my throat as they moved slowly ahead.

### Dohazari and Beyond — 1944:

One evening at dusk I followed a proper footpath winding up to the bamboo hospital at Dohazari. I wanted to visit a mate in with dysentery. He was very ill and a friendly face was always welcome, if only to cheer him up a bit. The night was calm and I could almost feel the trees and bushes breathing in the still night air. As I became aware of some presence near at hand, my instinct was alerted and on impulse I swung round piercing the night with a hand torch. The beam picked out two jackals stealthily converging from either side of the track about to grab my ankles! Instinctively I faced them blinding their eyes with the strong light and simultaneously kicking out in my best soccer tradition. The pair did not run away but melted back into the undergrowth. They resembled silver foxes in the brief glimpse I got of them; much smaller than the hyena which once slunk past me in the dead of night while I stood on guard duty during our first move south from Dohazari down the Arakan (November 1942).

The nurses stationed in the Dohazari-Comilla-type hospitals earned our eternal respect. The areas concerned were glorified swamps during the monsoon season with dirt floors and mosquito-infested bamboo walls and roofs (no ceilings); nor did they have any other mod cons. There were no off-duty places to go and should the staff wish to shop in the bazaar the army supplied escorts for security reasons.

Conditions for the troops were never first class either. An air force pilot once visited the front line positions in an unofficial capacity as he put it, just to see how the ground troops managed to exist in the hostile environment which engulfed such a vast jungle-clad area as seen from the air. He was intrigued about how his job compared with the overall ant-like scene far below. He had nothing but admiration for those he described as the unsung heroes, who were literally left to get on with the real war regardless of recognition. I replied that apart from the odd elephant trumpeting at night, always at a distance, the only other wildlife was the occasional snake which had been unearthed accidentally. He agreed that would be right enough as he often observed stampeding animals about twenty miles ahead of the shooting area. I realised that this pilot was concerned for his fellow man and to come all that way just to see for himself was truly a remarkable gesture. Like Lord Louis Mountbatten, he also came to see for himself!

## *Dohazari Airstrip — 1944:*

The railhead at Dohazari was defended from air attacks by Bofors ack-ack guns as there were no fighter planes capable of intercepting the Japanese formations which roamed the skies at will in our part of the world. Normally the formations consisted of twenty-seven twin-engined bombers which looked like German Dorniers with Bristol Pegasus engines, which in fact they were. The Japanese were renowned for copying and improving western technology, which they still do to this day. However, the enemy took their supremacy too much for granted, coming down to low levels and treating the punitive defences with contempt, before casually cruising back to base somewhere to the south, their aerobatics over for another day.

Late one afternoon there was great excitement at the local airstrip when preparations were hurriedly made to accommodate a squadron of Spitfires secretly flown in and camouflaged immediately around the perimeter. They were of the latest vintage and were probably Mk IVs. The stage was set for the next Japanese visit, which duly came within a day or so. Wireless outposts had been established covering the various approaches to our area thereby giving us an early warning system. Ack-ack guns were placed on strategic getaway routes along the valleys to the south; everyone was ready for the big event.

The eastern sun rose out of the clear morning sky. "Scramble! Action stations!" The Spitfires took to the air and were soon climbing swiftly into the sun, which was now rising high in the clear heavens above. I was reminded of Kipling's famous words: "Where the dawn comes up like thunder...." We were on the road to Mandalay in a manner of speaking too.

The Japs arrived, as usual circling the area at about 2,000 feet when, without warning, the Spitfires swooped down on them from out of the sun, shooting down fifteen of the enemy, and causing the rest to scatter in all directions. The chase was on and the Japs hurriedly headed south — right into a trap. The guns opening up on predicted ranges as the enemy crossed their line of fire. Every plane was destroyed. No Japanese survived and the British made no announcement to the outside world. The Japanese were stunned but curious.

Finally they made their move five days later when a lone reconnaissance plane poked its nose over the eastern ridge of the Lushai Hills to the north of the usual approach route. That plane was promptly shot down and it was later found to contain some VIP high-ranking Japanese General Staff, none of whom survived. So ended the saga of Japanese supremacy in the air in Burma at long last.

During the earlier part of 1943, few planes ventured down the Arakan other than Japanese. British patrols amounted to one Hurribomber converted for hit and run strafing duties, as at best they could barely exceed 240 mph and were no use as fighters in the tropical environment peculiar to that region. One pilot, on the regular 'milk run' down the coast to Akyab and back, had to make a forced landing on the beach behind our gun positions. The pilot thought he was down on enemy-held territory and as he climbed out of the cockpit he was armed to the teeth with side arms and prepared to die fighting as troops rushed towards him from the sand dunes! He soon found to his relief that the Japs didn't speak with a Scottish accent. The boys soon dragged the crippled plane well above high water and covered it with scrub to avoid detection from the air. The pilot got safely back to base travelling overland, and about a week later a salvage crew arrived to dismantle the Hurricane and took it back to base. I think their base was either Chittagong or Hatazari further north.

The same pilot later flew over our positions, circled, and dropped a large carton of cigarettes in gratitude, to be shared among the lads. He often waved to us on his return trips, flying above the waves at 'zero' feet to avoid detection by the Japs.

A story related to me later by an ack-ack gunner concerning that same pilot, is worthy of a mention. He was returning to base having used up all his ammo when he found the airstrip under attack from Japanese Zeros which were more than a match for his obsolete Hurricane. His fuel was running low with only fifteen minutes' flying time left. Down he went and deliberately provoked a Zero pilot to follow him down over the aerodrome in line with the Bofors ack-ack guns. The gunners got the message, let him through, and bagged the Zero now in their line of sight!

The Hurribomber pilot then landed safely minus his ammo and out of fuel, with one Japanese Zero shared with the gunners to his credit. A noble deed indeed!

Later we saw regular sorties, of a few dive bombers at a time, attempting to dislodge the Japs from their bunkers and tunnels in the foothills overlooking Donbaik. Those pilots were brave men. Some failed to pull out of their dives (probably hit). The attacks boosted our morale but the Japs remained invincible. We still had a lot to learn.

The first campaign was fraught with too little too late, poor lines of communications, and no navy or air transport to back up the beleaguered troops. Withdrawal before the monsoon was inevitable.

The ultimate line of defence was to the north of Maungdaw and east towards the Maungdaw and Buthidaung Tunnels, forming a triangle with Cox's Bazaar, later to be known as the Admin Box. This was a strategic defence post, which held out against repeated Japanese attacks from the south until the enemy finally withdrew after being overwhelmingly defeated at Kohima and Imphal.

Occupation troops gradually took over as the main advance went down the Chindwin and across to Mandalay, thereby avoiding the more hazardous coastal route to the south via Akyab and Ramree. Rangoon was to become a non-event in the latter stages of the war.

### Dohazari Witch Doctor — 1944:

The main and only road south from Chittagong passed through Dohazari and maintained a supply route to the Admin Box area where a confrontation with the enemy was contained over a long period of time, eventually culminating in stalemate as the main push finally emanated from Kohima and Imphal in the north.

During the constant movement of troops, several units passed our ack-ack camp adjacent to the road about a mile from the railhead. Among those troops were a large contingent of African units. It was there one evening, while on guard duty at our ammo hut constructed of bamboo, that I had an unusual encounter with a handful of tall, arrogant and mischievous rankers, dressed in colonial drill uniforms and wearing special army boots designed for barefoot people who'd never worn shoes in their lives before, and whose feet were large, broad and flat with spread-out toes. They made conversation until they became a nuisance.

As a sentry should not be distracted from his duty, I requested them to move on. In reply I was asked if I would shoot if they refused! By this time they were joined by a slightly shorter African also in drill uniform. He seemed to have an aura which commanded reverence and respect, and soon became their spokesman. I soon realised he was well-educated and could have passed for a minister of religion. His remarks became more subtle, which put me further on guard. He dared me to shoot him, assuring me that bullets would not harm him! His audience started to goad me and I realised I could fall into a cunning trap. The witch doctor knew I wouldn't shoot, and because of that, carried out the pretence to convince his spellbound followers. He had made his point, I wanted to shoot him, but broke his spell by shouting "Turn out the guard!" They turned tail with the witch doctor backing away less hurriedly. He knew I had tumbled to his little game. I could never forget such a unique situation for the rest of my life.

I was assured later that those primitive-minded troops did have their witch doctors on the strength and that the rhino whip was common punishment for defaulters lined up on the parade ground! I once watched them feeding by the roadside. They produced a large, square biscuit tin and emptied a seven-pound tin of bully beef into it then a seven-pound tin of syrup and stirred the mixture into a stew. It was heated over a fire, then devoured. They were like animals in a zoo, devoid of all table manners. The Indian villagers dreaded them as they had no respect for women or animals and grabbed what took their fancy and left the inhabitants in a state of terror.

Discipline was lacking and they were classed as unreliable even among their own white officers and NCOs. The least scare caused them to vanish from the scene, leaving perhaps their white patrol leader very much out on his own, as was once related to me while in Loretto Hospital by a very fortunate sergeant who lived to tell the tale.

## Dohazari — 1944:

With the Japanese losing the supremacy of the air over the Arakan, the need for ack-ack batteries lessened and High Command decided to leave the secondary defence to Indian units as white troops could be more strategically deployed. This move soon became evident when the 2nd British Division (all white) took the brunt of the Japanese onslaught at Kohima along with other supporting units. For various reasons there were many casualties, and reinforcements were needed urgently. The only white reserves were anti-aircraft personnel who were suddenly made redundant and posted northeast to Dimapur, there to be directed to whatever units could use their military expertise. In many instances they had very little training for infantry or other combat commitments and many were medically graded other than A1.

The British Army needed the men, and it was obvious that the Medical Corps had to obey orders just like any other mob. All personnel under thirty-five possessing all four limbs and still breathing, were promptly upgraded to A1 and posted forthwith after visiting one solitary colonel in Chittagong. He was a discredit to his profession and sat there, tongue in cheek, virtually stamping out everyone A1 regardless. It was rumoured that he got a fifty rupee bonus for all he passed. He looked mean enough to me and obviously didn't care for the health and welfare of the men, or the front-line units who had to accept them. Many men who qualified for the Burma Star never saw the front line, while others were repeatedly sent back to their front-line units in a continuous stream, firstly to hospital then to return via the various staging camps to relive the privations and humiliation of a deprived but ever-sensitive human being. It would have been a great boost to morale if we had been treated with a little more dignity and respect by those who had the authority invested in them.

Before leaving Dohazari, we had a visiting padre call on us. He was a rather young lad, who stressed to us the importance of good morale and pointed out that it was high time we broke away from our mother's apron strings and realised that there was a war to be fought and won against a pagan enemy. He implied that all those other than Christians should be wiped off the face of the earth! I had been away from home two and a half years by then and our padre approximately three months. He was slightly older than me but I claimed to know more about the enemy than he did. He played a few gramophone records, 'Home Sweet Home', etc., to cheer us up! The lads started to cry aloud and he didn't like our reaction. One man offered to swap his rifle and bayonet for his gramophone and jeep, but the padre gave up his crusade, packed his gear and left the camp the same night! No doubt he had no wish to fight the enemy alone.

My next move was to Dimapur, travelling by rail through Comilla then through the Ghats into the foothills of Assam. I remember sitting in the train by a siding as an American engine tried to negotiate a gradient with great difficulty while hauling a heavy train load of supplies to the front-line railhead. The wheels were spinning as the roaring clouds of steam hissed from the steel monster. Another engine nudged it to the top of the rise in order to clear the way for the following train, which was being hauled by a British Garret class engine with articulated front and rear driving units, and powered by a conventional steam-boiler assembly. It was not very elegant perhaps, but highly suited to the task before it. It was with deep pride that I watched the locomotive virtually walk up that gradient with an equally massive load.

During my short stay at Dimapur I watched the huge American bulldozers gouge out the base of the massive teak trees prior to raising their 'blade' and pushing them over like matchsticks, in order to clear away an area for billets and supply dumps. Our billet was a long bamboo basha, which would sleep around forty men with a door either end. I was invited to play with a few intellectuals, who taught me the game of contract bridge, which was fascinating and we played virtually all night. During the evening there was a commotion as the WO came yelling through the hut running for his life, followed by a boozed-up private, lunging behind wielding a rifle and bayonet and shouting, "I'll get the bastard!" I don't think he did, I suspect he finished up in the guard room where he sobered up.

The Brigade HQ Intelligence officer liked my Scottish accent and asked me if I would like to be a Royal Scot. I promptly said no. Having been given no other option I was then told to report to Battalion HQ at Kohima. I had offered to go to the Royal Artillery or, as a second choice, the Royal Signals. Again I was frustrated by the indignity of arrogant military indifference. I was a highly trained signaller and above the standard required for infantry, but my opinion didn't count in the logic of military thinking. I duly reported to the Royal Scots (lst Battalion) shortly after they had taken a vital role in the battle of Kohima, losing many men and were depleted in numbers as a consequence with many sick and wounded.

Wisps of smoke were still rising from the battle area, where stunted trees highlighted the landscape. The various units had buried their dead and were now sheltering from the intermittent rain, sheltered by bamboo huts propped against the hillsides. These huts had no doubt been erected by Naga natives who were staunch allies and hated the Japanese invaders.

I was welcomed by the men and they seemed especially pleased as they had seen action down the Arakan when attached to our Brigade. They were known as the 6th Independent Infantry Brigade and had earlier seen service in Madagascar before continuing on to India. Those men were the salt of the earth, they were real soldiers and had a different outlook on life. They stuck together in small individual groups or cliques, which was difficult for an outsider like myself to understand at first. They also put a strong emphasis on parochial interests such as "what lodge do you belong to?"

### Air Ambulance to Comilla — 1944:

Shortly after joining the Royal Scots at Kohima, I had a relapse of malaria and was sent up the long, winding road to the military hospital at Imphal. All of us were checked in and were given blood tests. The results later showed a blood count deficiency of around 50% below normal, i.e. a reading of about 300, when normal was around 600. In simple terms this meant we were suffering from malnutrition and were open to any disease kicking around.

At that time typhus was the number one killer and very few survived the ordeal. It was contracted from lice-ridden rats feeding on dead carcases. The lice brushed off the rats on to the long grass and were transmitted to humans walking through the undergrowth. The victims of typhus had a long crisis spell which took its toll on the underfed constitution and only the fittest survived. We had to wear long-sleeved bush jackets and slacks, sponged daily with insect repellent, and tight puttee bandages were wrapped round our ankles sealing the tops of our boots to prevent lice and leeches from getting near the flesh. The often-stifling heat in the combat area added to our overall discomfort, which in turn, did nothing to boost our morale.

As casualties kept on arriving we were duly sent over to the airstrip to await air transport which would take us to Comilla Military Hospital. The plane duly arrived to pick us up. It was a US Army DC3 Dakota with a crew of three, who seemed to go about their task in a casual, nonchalant manner with the characteristic American habit of chewing gum. Slowly we were checked in as we boarded the DC3, then the hatch door was closed and the plane taxied to the end of the dust-blown runway. The runway had a limited distance, which meant the load factors were critical. As there had been the odd fatal crash caution could not be ignored. Our pilot gradually increased the engine revs until the two air-cooled motors were straining on their mountings. The whole plane vibrated in a continuous shudder until the pilot was given the thumbs-up sign from the ground crew. "Chocks Away!" The engines screamed on full power and we soon began to hurtle along the runway into the wind. The hills ahead were looming towards us faster by the second. One more heave and we were airborne! The plane veered to starboard as we started the long slow climb which would take us above the peaks of the Assam mountain ranges extending from the mighty Himalayas towering away to the west and north.

We were told we could smoke and sit anywhere and I chose to sit near the wireless operator, from where I could watch the radar beam on the small round cathode tube.

The engines on the DC3 were close to the fuselage mounted on the roots of the slightly flexible wings. As I glanced through a port window, fascinated by the experience of my first ever flight, I noticed short flames spluttering from the engine cowling. I panicked as I pointed the wireless operator towards the motor. He grinned as he coolly grabbed the extinguisher, which had a long nozzle, and promptly pointed it through a small hole in line with the motor dousing the flames almost instantly. He then explained it was a common occurrence and we were not in any real danger, which was a relief for yours truly. We flew at between nine and ten thousand feet. My ears became blocked and it became colder as I continued to watch the radar beam once more. Suddenly the plane lurched violently to starboard as the beam vanished from the tube. We banked sharply as I looked towards the operator for an explanation. He quickly pointed to our left as we veered away from a solid mass of menacing black cloud, and said "Ice. We couldn't tackle that and it is too high to climb over, so we will circle till we are back on the beam again!"

The plane steadied back on course as we gradually descended to a warmer altitude leaving the mountains behind us. Comilla was not far away. Slowly we began to circle in a wide arc until finally an airstrip could be seen in a clearing among the Bengal palms and scrub far below. One more circle and the pilot decided to land. As we approached the strip we seemed a bit high, so I assumed we would overshoot and come round again. But no — halfway along the runway the wheels bounced, then quite a shaky touchdown. The plane rocked as it rolled fast along the shortened strip. We could see the flaps working overtime and felt the brakes surging as the pilot attempted to pull up. Suddenly there was an almighty heave on the brakes just before the plane veered and lurched to the right as a forest of palm trees loomed at the extreme end of the small airstrip. We had stopped at last, the crew were more puzzled than the passengers.

During the brief silence that followed, a solitary RAF figure approached us from a bamboo hut on the fringe of the jungle to enquire about our flight plan. When asked if we were at Comilla, he replied, "No, this is an emergency fighter strip only. Comilla is thirty-six miles west of here, and you can't take off from here with that load!" We were duly disembarked and sent on to hospital by truck along a dusty and bumpy road to the mud and bamboo shanty town of Comilla. The Dakota returned to its base at Dum-Dum near Calcutta.

After admission to Comilla Hospital, I awoke one night around 1.30 a.m. in a state of frenzy, my whole body 'aflame' and completely covered with blisters. The experience was frightening and unprecedented. The night orderly was alarmed and called out the duty medical officer along with the night sister, who had me rolled in a blanket and promptly taken to the ablution building. I was soon surrounded by concerned staff. The senior nurse ordered a zinc bath and all the ice and ice water available, at the double! I was stripped and plunged in to the freezing water and doused with countless jugs of bath water over my head until my whole body temperature dropped to near normal. The shock nearly killed me as I felt like a very frightened animal. As I stood up eventually in the bath, several hands applied layers of calamine lotion to my fast-drying skin (caused by the still warm internal body heat). The calamine was also very cooling and as I shivered in the wet surroundings fresh, clean pyjamas were put on my wet, plastered body. Then I was immediately wheeled back to the ward and tucked snugly into bed.

I slept well, but in the morning I told my mate in the next bed about a nightmare I had had. He looked at me puzzled, then slowly started to grin a little. "You don't remember, do you?"

I looked back at him puzzled. "What do you mean?"

He replied, "It was no bloody nightmare, Jock! You woke up the whole ward and you were the only one that slept when they brought you back."

So it was true after all. I then noticed my pyjamas were starchy with dried calamine powder, but not a blemish could be seen on my whole body. The doctor and sister could offer no explanation except to say that as no one else was affected it was not food poisoning. In the end it was put down to some allergy peculiar to yours truly. My skin was allergic to many irritants such as woollen army shirts, underwear and soap, etc., (so perhaps there was a link somewhere). I tried to wear cotton shirts under my uniform whenever possible. Sheets and pyjamas were not issued or allowed in the British Army, but the navy and air force enjoyed a more civilised status. My career in the army was never comfortable, but like all the rest of the boys we just had to soldier on. Roll on civvy street!

## *Assam and Chindwin — 1944-45:*

Having spent a short spell in dock at Imphal and Comilla with malaria, I then reported to the nearest staging camp (Kanglatomi Area) where the WO in charge of transport asked me to volunteer as driver to a bunch of roughnecks who were to travel south and join up with a sapper unit involved in forward operations such as demolishing mines, throwing across pontoon bridges, etc. We were ferrying new vehicles to the forward troops and I was to rejoin the Royal Scots anyway. It seemed an amicable arrangement, so we set off the next morning at first light. Rations and petrol were to be picked up en route. I was briefly introduced to my travelling companions and we (seven of us) set off south.

One man, who was the obvious leader, sat up front with me. He turned out to be a fellow Scot and also had red hair. He took to me right away and to him I was the 'pinnacle of perfection'. I felt unworthy of the title until he unfolded his story and that of his companions: they had been released from Lucknow Military Prison on the condition that they 'volunteered' for front-line duty, which they did gladly. They had all been sentenced to prison for violent crimes such as manslaughter! It was hard to believe, but I had their word for it. I soon found that they all had one thing in common: they rebelled against the army's brand of discipline, and reacted like captive animals in a cage. To me those men were the very essence of adventurous British manhood: proud, confident and daring to tackle the unknown, born free to run free. They were driven to an environment hostile to them and rebelled, only to suffer the humiliating consequences. Again I blamed the men who misused their rank to get at those men. Simply, their superiors had panicked with fear, and threw the book at them for revenge, thereby making them enemies to society and branding them for life as criminals.

We negotiated the winding track through mountainous gorges, traversing a pathway of fallen rocks, thick layers of powdered dust, and narrow, overhanging drops of many thousands of feet to the valleys far below. We were travelling through the Tamu section in the direction of Kabaw Valley, named Death Valley by some, situated in a region between the Manipur and Chindwin Ranges. Some drivers who drove during the blackout in Britain used to complain about using masked headlights! We had to drive at dust intervals in the dark without lights, except perhaps a very deceptive moonlight whose shadows could be very misleading. Most army drivers had to rely entirely on an illuminated white spot on the diff of the vehicle in front; if one driver got lost, the following vehicles did likewise!

After many hours' travelling, it was now dark. We had eaten the last of our rations, which were simply bread and jam. It was time to replenish our supplies at the nearest supply depot, which was hard to find at around 1.30 in the morning.

We finally found an obscure sign depicting the supply dump we had been looking for. In the dark, it was difficult to see any form of life, so we proceeded to investigate and wandered into a compound where we were halted by an Indian sentry (Army Service Corps). The lad was nervous and very young, but agreed to lead us to his 'officer sahib', who was sleeping in a bamboo basha on a rise overlooking the dump entrance. When awakened, the white officer was not impressed with our presence. However, we asked for food and a bed for the night, explaining our mission. He refused point blank, seemed agitated and suffering from an overdose of gin, and ordered us off the premises! The sentry was uneasy with his rifle and fixed bayonet, so one of my mates disarmed him and the rest of my squad suddenly adopted an angry attitude through the tactless folly of the first lieutenant. We expected courtesy and co-operation, but were frustrated by a pompous, half-drunk apology for a British officer.

The situation became tense. My mates were in an angry mood and the officer had left himself at the mercy of desperate men. My cool, logical brain had to diffuse the situation fast! I exercised what charisma the lads held in me and bluffed my way into a compromise. I asked the officer for petrol to set us on our way, and suggested that perhaps we could sort things out in the morning in the light of day. I appeared to give in easily. My mates seemed puzzled, but backed off. They saw I was against violence, but I also indicated that I had a plan.

We were escorted through the gate and back to the truck with four tins of petrol. The boy sentry was given back his rifle and we set off slowly round the next blind bend where I pulled up by the outer perimeter of the sprawling dump site. The lads got the message, crawled through the wire and rummaged quietly among the stockpiles, while I stood guard by the truck. The boys helped themselves to seven-pound tins of bully beef, whole potatoes, tinned fruit cocktail, smaller tins of blackcurrant jam, bacon rashers, and army biscuits — enough to last the rest of our journey. Our actions were of necessity — not criminal. Every good soldier carried a survival kit. We had all left our mothers' apron strings long long ago and I'm sure they would have been proud of us!

We crawled down the road and, within half an hour, found a small stream just off the road where we lit a fire, had a meal and bedded down for the rest of the night. It was broad daylight when the boys woke me up with a mug of tea, biscuits and bacon, followed by fruit cocktail! We all had a soldier's bath in the stream using the four-gallon square biscuit tin as a bucket to pour water over our heads. The boys cleaned out the truck and we set off towards the Kabaw Valley.

The road seemed to consist of bomb craters filled with dust. I circumnavigated them whenever I could, but where we were liable to get stuck, the lads hopped out of the back of the truck and bodily heaved it across — otherwise we would sink to the axles.

We experienced trouble with condensation and silt in the petrol even though the tins were sealed and soldered. Fortunately, a lot of water and silt was stopped in the large filter bowl on the fuel line before the petrol passed through the pump unit into the carburettor. I got caught the first time and had to strip the whole lot, but afterwards stopped at regular intervals and cleaned the filter bowl, which was always needing attention. I made replacement gaskets from the lads' playing cards, starting with the joker! It did the trick.

The valley was heavily wooded with teak and scrub. One section was cut in a long, broad surveyed path to accommodate telegraph poles and a future road heading south, but it would be completed long after we had advanced along the old road to Mandalay.

The rest of our journey was uneventful until we found the road blocked by a few vehicles ahead. One had apparently slipped over the side of a sloping bank. No one seemed to know what to do, so I took over by asking a wrecker-truck (jib) driver to back up and haul the truck out. He replied that he couldn't operate the winch! I got into the cab, tried a few levers, got the system and reversed the truck with the jib overhanging the sloping bank. I lowered the winch rope, took up the slack, told the ditched truck driver to keep his wheels turning slowly and between us, we walked the truck back on to the road. There were three cheers all round, then each vehicle continued independently once more. I don't remember seeing an officer or NCO throughout the whole trip on that convoy, yet we all got there without the red tape associated with so-called army discipline.

On arrival at the transport distributing area, I was directed by an MP into a huge parking lot completely hidden by tall elephant grass. It was a unique experience driving on flattened basket-weave matting with a maze of individual bays branching off in all directions. The very high, very thick grass seemed to suggest that we were suspended on top of a swamp. I handed over the truck and remaining rations and rejoined the Royal Scots camped down the road. It must have been close to Christmas as they were having an early Christmas dinner, specially provided by Army HQ. This was because we were due to move south and across the Chindwin around Christmas and New Year (1944-45). The army did a fine job with the catering and produced a surprising amount of exotic food to brighten up a very sombre situation, which was in essence the atmosphere surrounding any unit prior to going into battle.

My travelling companions said their farewells at the transport depot. We promised to meet again at a later date and celebrate our bond of friendship. Such is war. The last I heard of them was that they were building pontoons across the Chindwin and later threw another bridge across a river under heavy enemy fire at Tada-U, south of Mandalay. I remember the latter occasion well.

The new intake now officially attached to the Royal Scots were to be tested in the use of small arms and were duly taken into the scrub. A range was set up and each of us was given ten rounds of .303 ammo and target cards to fire at. My turn came round so I lay prostrate on the ground, loaded the Lee-Enfield and took aim.

"Stop!" yelled the sergeant-major, "you'll break your bloody jaw. It's obvious you've never fired a rifle in your life!"

I looked up at him angrily and asked what was wrong.

He replied with a few choice words that you can't fire a rifle from the right shoulder and sight it with the left eye!

I yelled at him in reply, "Put up that target. I'll show you something!"

He let me go ahead, saying that even if I could fire successfully I'd never hit the target, and that I'd have to keep on firing till I could prove otherwise!

I had a 'telescopic' left eye and had every confidence in my proficiency as a marksman. I took casual aim and, as the bull came into view, held my breath and gently squeezed the trigger, repeating the action ten times. I then asked to see the target, but the SM wouldn't let me. I was told later that every one was an inner. I did not have to fire again, though many others did.

During that episode some of the intake were being instructed on how to throw grenades nearby, and an instructor was killed while heroically trying to get rid of someone's mistake. The pin had been carelessly removed, or the grenade had not been thrown clear. One thing came through to me at that place: we were looked upon as a rather dumb lot — no doubt with some justification. On the other hand, my knowledge of signalling was advanced compared with infantry standards and I felt ill at ease at times as I was always open to criticism from my opposite numbers. I could cope with that but although I respected every one of them I later discovered that the signals officer was my only concern. He was a gong hunter and had little time for the likes of a shell-shocked gunner, such as me.

Being an infantryman was not my bag. The privates were treated like third-grade illiterate ex-borstal delinquents, while the NCOs over-patronised their immediate superiors. I was soon to discover that we had a fine bunch of officers (bar one) and the RSM was allowed to run the battalion as he pleased. The whole set up could be compared to what one reads about the French Foreign Legion. I was not afraid of any of them, but I expected to be treated like a human being, which was the case in the Royal Artillery. I was always told that respect had to be earned, and it is still a good maxim. One must remember that the 1st Royal Scots were the most senior infantry regiment in the British Army and known as the First of Foot! This traditional claim was not made lightly and only the Royal Artillery were senior to them — a sore point in any tradition-soaked regular soldier. My comrades and I represented something which had little meaning to us, but which was a thorn in the flesh to the indoctrinated — i.e. the RSM and his bootlickers. When a comrade falls by the wayside while on the march in a dried-up tropical dust bowl you stop momentarily and give him a drink from your water bottle and place him in the shade. Our RSM forbade it and the victim was left to survive, hopefully, until the Red Cross found him perhaps the next day.

### A Dental Distraction:

I was badly in need of dental treatment and duly reported to our battalion medical officer who referred me to a field dentist. Next morning I set off on the ration truck to an unknown destination. The driver pulled up miles from nowhere and pointed to a half-hidden track flanked with thick bushes, wishing me all the best! As I walked forward I came to a clearing with a bamboo hut overlooking the surrounding landscape of trees and scrub. I noticed a sporting rifle leaning against the wall with the butt resting on the verandah, and I yelled out "Is there anyone at home?"

A voice boomed out, "Yes! Just come in, will you. I won't be long."

The dentist soon appeared and gave me a great welcome as if we'd been friends for years, in spite of his rank (captain, I think). He had a soft spot for Scotsmen — perhaps his mother was a Scot. The whole scene inside was primitive and the drill was driven by foot pedal!

On examination it was decided that I needed seven fillings, so I volunteered to have them done all in one go. I did not want to repeat the long journey back again along the bumpy, dust-laden bush track at least two hours' drive from our camp. Besides, the battalion was sure to move on at a moment's notice — we were well south of the Chindwin by then. The dentist chatted away to me as he pushed his foot on the pedal, the drill grinding away in a sickening whine. I detested the primitive treatment, but enjoyed the operator's sense of humour. He was about thirtyish and a fine-looking bloke, but I could find no logic to why this spot was chosen as a dental centre. However the guy was apparently happy at his work and seemed to enjoy his lonely posting.

The reader may find such an event hard to swallow but, to continue regardless, after each and every filling, the dentist (or captain) took a short break from his work, stretched his legs outside, grabbed the rifle on the verandah and took a shot at one of the numerous crow-like birds which nested among the high trees across the neglected lawn where there was an incessant din from the rookery. His shooting was accurate and he must have bagged one each time he took a break away from the treadle machine. He said it relieved the boredom and helped to keep the over-populated crows under control.

I left the clearing more puzzled than when I first entered. The truck picked me up somewhere along the dusty track on the way back to camp. Needless to say, I could never forget such a melodramatic interlude from reality. Fact is stranger than fiction.

The dentist told me that the treatment would have cost me twenty guineas in London! But, we weren't in London — it could hardly be classed as Harley Street either!

## Across the Chindwin — 1945:

We marched like true infantrymen all the way, wherever we went, and the road south was long and dusty. It was the dry season and many rivers and creeks were dried up, but the Chindwin wasn't! We crossed by barge, as either the pontoons were not ready for us or the river was running too high. On the far side we soon found the abandoned relics of war left by that gallant band of men forced to retreat before the advancing 'invincible' Japanese Army back in late 1941/early1942. There were trucks and 3.7 ack-ack guns. All had been immobilised and the latter spiked in true artillery fashion. They had reached the end of the road and I was surprised they had brought the guns so far, no doubt with a great amount of difficulty as the way ahead was a dead end. However, many years later I spoke to a medical officer who had come that way with the refugees. He said that they forded the rivers with elephants, which eventually carried them over the mountains into India. Very few survived the ordeal. The elephants climbed the steep slopes on their knees!

One day we camped in a dried-up riverbed, but found water by scooping out holes in the gravel. We all took turns at having a bath as we were filthy with dust and sweat. Our clothes were bleached by the sun and every man was hungry. Soon we heard the familiar sound of Dakota transport planes and everyone's morale soared with thoughts of food. The planes circled, spotted us, and the crew kicked out bales of fodder for the mules! I asked the CO about our rations, but he shrugged his shoulders and said, "Maybe tomorrow, if they can find us." We moved on the next day, hoping they would.

Our march south was tough going and it was later decided to travel by night as our dust cloud could be seen for miles and the heat was sapping the strength from even the fittest. We were on short rations and suffering from heat exhaustion, but the pace was relentlessly maintained. We stopped for a rest along the east bank of the Chindwin one day, and were given a reasonable meal while an officer went round handing out brown aspirin-shaped pills. We swallowed them like good soldiers. Then I heard the MO tell the officer, "For God's sake don't give them those too often, or I won't be held responsible." They were pep pills and after a few hours' sleep we got up at dusk and marched all night at a fast gallop. Next day the lack of sleep caught up with us and we flaked out, utterly exhausted.

I hate to think how many miles we were marching each day; it was a colossal amount. When we finally arrived outside Shwebo we were met by the Cameron Highlanders who piped us into the assembly area with rousing cheers. A VIP congratulated us on our march and stated that we had saved 32,000 gallons of petrol for the war effort! Someone from the audience retorted by pointing out we had lost an equal amount in sweat!

We took up tactical positions from then on as the enemy was not too far in front making a continuous strategic withdrawal towards the big river. As we left Shwebo I saw a Dakota taking off from the newly captured airstrip having unloaded vital supplies and returning with wounded. Two Jap Zeros swooped down on the helpless plane and shot it out of the sky while only a few hundred feet above the ground, and it crashed in a sickening pall of smoke. As far as I could see there would be no survivors. We marched on in single file either side of the road accompanied by about four General Lee tanks.

During one of our routine wayside halts, we happened to stop at a native hut just off the road. I spotted an Indian civilian who came forward when I said a few words in Hindustani to him. I asked if he had any tomatoes or other fruit and he salaamed, returned to the house and brought me a wee basket of lovely ripe tomatoes. He was young and intelligent and told me that the Japs were waiting for us round the next curve about a mile down the road. I thanked him and told the signals officer who was unconvinced by my message and told me, "Get back to the ranks and don't speak with the natives!" This attitude raised my hackles and I demanded to see the CO, but he changed his mind and told the chief himself. The CO took the necessary precautions and one company was sent ahead. Sure enough, the Japs opened up as they cautiously rounded the bend. One man was killed and later a tank got hit with an AP shell before the following tank destroyed the Jap gun hidden by the deep monsoon drain at the side of the road, the muzzle level with the road itself. I had recognised marks of steel-rimmed gun wheels earlier, but who would listen to an observant artilleryman? The enemy was finally flushed out and we moved ahead once more the next day. We were still following wheel marks of guns which appeared to have been hauled manually. Being called and treated like an idiot I kept my observations to myself, hoping the bosses would have noticed them too. We rounded another bend and two fast-reloading guns opened up on us but we were on the alert by now and well spread out.

I remember a tree which caught my eye as we were taking cover prior to rushing into a wooded village. It was an unnatural, vivid green and the gunfire finally disclosed that the tree was clustered with beautiful green parakeets as they rose into the air in a flight of panic. I was scared stiff myself at the time so we shared a lot in common. One of the wee birds was later presented to the padre in a home-made cage by one of the lads.

We continued towards Sagaing and finally took up positions on high ground overlooking the inside elbow of the Irrawaddy river. To the left was the steel-girdered bridge destroyed earlier, but pointing the way to

70

Mandalay in the east. Our route led towards Ywathigy to the west where the Japs made a last ditch stand before retreating to the south bank of the big river.

### Ywathigy Air Strike — 1945:

The army was getting organised at long last and we encountered our first ever mobile bath unit just before Ywathigy. We were paraded down to a wood and saw how, by a great deal of ingenuity, the engineers at base workshops had cut oil drums longways in half to make bathtubs, and set up a hot water unit. The mobile squad set up screens, laid tarpaulins on a sloping forest floor for drainage and were in business. As we walked in we stepped out of our filthy, greasy, oil-impregnated uniforms, grabbed a towel and sat down in a steaming hot tub to soak away years of sweat and grime. Then we came out the other end and into clean second-hand jungle slacks and bush jackets, with clean vests and pants. We even saw a few films on the outdoor movies (forerunner of the drive-ins of today), during the odd spell in a rest area.

As we moved towards Ywathigy the guns of other units were making themselves heard further west. At long last we were no longer alone, and the Japs were on the run everywhere. The Royal Scots were directed to attack Ywathigy when waves of American B25 (Mitchell) bombers were observed flying west to east towards Mandalay. We did not know that they were our support aircraft as they appeared more like a ceremonial fly-past over Hollywood, USA! They did not appear to identify their targets, but promptly jettisoned their bombs not far from our HQ, from an altitude of around 5,000 feet minimum! Needless to add that they missed the target assigned to them and overshot the area by about 350 yards! We received many casualties and the tank crews were as demoralised as we were. The attack had to be called off and the ground commanders had a hurried rethink of the whole situation. We were all reassured that the RAF would take over the next strike, which they meticulously did.

The RAF commander came down personally and obtained first-hand information from the army commanders on the spot, identifying each specific bunker from aerial photographs. Next morning the Brylcreem Boys came over and spotted each individual target assigned to them, while their CO was on the ground with us, using a jeep fitted with a ground-to-air transmitter. He called in each pilot in turn and told them to attack only when they were sure of their targets. Then down they came in single file. Our morale soared as those magnificent men in their flying machines flew right down to zero feet, every bomb a bull's-eye. Then they all came round again, emptying their guns at any Japs making a run for the river bank.

We were proud to be British on that memorable occasion. I think the RAF flew Thunderbolts on that mission and Mosquitos were used to patrol the river day and night prior to our battalion crossing to the south bank in

71

DUKWs. Incidentally, I had my picture taken on that occasion by an official War Office correspondent. There were three of us returning to HQ after being chased by a sniper hidden up among the trees at the height of the battle. I was later shown the photograph in a paperback picture magazine called *Campaign Burma*.

## Across the Irrawaddy — 1945

The Royal Scots routed the Japs from their last foothold on the north bank of the Irrawaddy, thanks to the valuable assistance of the RAF who also strafed the enemy as they attempted to cross to the south bank. Many never made it.

We crossed the mighty river in pursuit, but met only a token resistance. From the other side, at our bridgehead, I watched a Taylor spotter plate plotting a convoy of Jap trucks fleeing in disarray. The artillery were putting down a barrage to hinder their progress. For a moment I felt like an OP signaller and understood all that was going on from past experience with the gunners. The shells were slow to arrive and rocket-firing planes would have been more appropriate on such a fast-moving target. Most of the Japs got clean away as a result.

The battalion advanced and captured the area uphill from the river, and we consolidated our positions for the night among the trees and scrub. The score was twenty-five Japs for the loss of one of ours. There was a deep well nearby where we had a wash and a meal and I cleaned my teeth! Soon after, the colonel and the MO came round and told us not to drink the water from the well as the Japs had dropped three bodies into it. I said, "Sorry, you are too late, but the water did have a queer, salty taste!" We had no ill effects from our experience as all our inoculations, etc. must have neutralised any disease from the water.

During the night, the enemy sent over an intermittent salvo of 150mm shells travelling over a range of 12-15,000 yards. I lay awake listening to the barely audible discharge, mentally timing the flight of the projectile and its maximum trajectory, then the descent as it lost velocity towards the target area. Luckily they were 300 yards to our right, obviously firing on a fixed map-reference bearing. I turned over and fell asleep. All was well.

During and apart from the trials and tribulations of an ordinary infantry signaller, there was an even more frightening battle going on within myself. It was one which was difficult to contain at times, making me feel totally lost and mentally confused as my body was receiving incoherent signals from my normally high-IQ brain, causing more confusion than ever. I briefly lost all co-ordination during those lapses, no doubt instigated by the earlier effects of shell-shock in the Arakan, back in January 1943, coupled with battle fatigue and general physical weakness. Lying out all night on listening watch did not induce mentally healthy sleep either, but as the rest of the men were enduring the same conditions, I could not complain. I pitied the front-line troops who had to put up with bomb-happy blokes like us, for there were others like me who had suffered from concussion because of shell or bomb blasts in previous campaigns. We soldiered on despite our affliction. Some might have called us brave men if they could have shared our misery. Many old soldiers understood the problem and treated the situation as another phase in the battle for survival. No one comes out unscathed, mentally or physically.

We were all blood brothers in a fiendish war. The enemy gave no quarter and fought with fanatical courage. I was close to becoming a Royal Scot as we shared a lot in common in those dark, weary months deep in the heart of Burma. I finally donned the Balmoral, which the CO had the tailor make for us out of a US Army blanket, with shiny red cotton lining. I reverently laid away the Royal Artillery forage cap with one word on the badge — *ubique* (Latin for everywhere) — very apt in my case.

Returning home was every soldier's dream. Our tank crews and Royal Signals personnel attached to us had been out east longer than any other units because their specialised skills were difficult to replace, so the army said! Those men were utterly demoralised and no one seemed to care a damn for their welfare. A message to all units came through, stating that personnel who had been out not more than two and a half years, would qualify for home leave to Britain as follows: one month travelling, followed by one month at home and one month to return! Those over that term of duty need not apply. So most of us had to soldier on regardless, and many never saw Blighty again. They were denied their last right on this earth, thanks to War Office backroom logic. We dutifully remained soldiers of the 'Forgotten Army', and had become used to such treatment.

Prior to swinging east towards Tada-U, I was given a walkie-talkie, which was approximately ten inches by six by four. The box was strapped high on my chest while the power pack hung at the rear on my web harness. We were to sweep an area ahead of us in order to flush out enemy pockets covering their retreat. My position was close to a Lee tank and I was told to maintain radio silence. I had a larynx microphone strapped round my throat, and headphones under my steel helmet, so I was pretty well tied up in my work! We had not gone far when I spotted a single telephone wire running up into a tree. It immediately dawned on me that earth return could be achieved by driving the earth spike into the sap while up the tree. Knowing what the signals officer's remarks would be, I said nothing as in his eyes, I was too dumb to think intelligently, though deep down I felt I could lose him on the science of military communications, for I too was a specialist in my field. My talents were being wasted in the infantry but that was not my fault.

Soon the 105mm shells were dropping around us. As we moved position the shelling pattern moved with us, and it became immediately obvious to me that it was an observed shoot and that tree was their OP. However we were now ahead of it and the Japs were behind us sitting pretty. Their gunners were on target all the way. Ironically I had to admire their skill and cunning. We all instinctively dived as the shells burst on impact on the dry, hard earth virtually all around us. My wireless prevented me from grovelling closer to Mother Earth and I was exposed more than necessary. Unknown to me, my aerial must have gone adrift in one of my many dives, but I failed to notice it at the time.

During the heat of battle, in order to make ourselves less conspicuous to the enemy, we were signalled to spread out. I became separated from the tanks while the company dispersed into small groups moving towards a wooded copse across a small valley, thereby completing a full circle. On carrying out those instructions, I stumbled across two wounded comrades who were dazed and wandering in the wrong direction. They asked where the first-aid unit was. I saw they needed help and I indicated the way towards company HQ on the edge of the perimeter. Just then another shell came over and we dived as it hit the earth right beside us, spinning madly. This was it! Our number was definitely on this one as it whined in our ears. It was a dud! I couldn't believe our luck as it finally lost momentum and skeetered away at an obtuse angle from us.

I helped my walking wounded to their feet after the shelling died down and we manoeuvred our way back to the perimeter using as much scrub for cover as possible. A shell landed at the top of the rise inside battalion territory. I later learned that it hit a canvas water butt at a company cookhouse. As we moved nearer the perimeter the signals officer came towards us and roared like a madman at me. "Where is your bloody aerial!" It was only then that I realised it was missing. "You'll be court martialled for deliberately throwing it away!" I was stunned by his remark. Only a rotten fiend could make such an accusation. I tried to explain, but he was in a blind rage. The man had obviously lost control of himself and that was noticeable in his snarling profile. "Get back to your position, you stupid idiot!" He then grabbed a rod from a No. 18 set or similar, pushed it in the shallow socket of my walkie-talkie and sent me on my way. I wanted to tell him about the Jap OP as we could still have got them, but I felt as if he had stuck a knife in my back. I was deeply in shock but I mechanically retraced my steps and met up with the main body who were returning in my direction carrying a dead comrade. I did not recognise who he was, all I remember was seeing the neat rows of nails on the soles of his boots as he was carried feet first. The company commander quietly told me I should have waited at the perimeter, as we had done what we had set out to do. He was a gentleman and we all respected him.

The signals officer had hurt me deeply with his sneering remarks, so I went to the MO and told him the whole history of my complaint and of the final insult to my integrity regarding the throwing away of my aerial, that I could never contemplate. He listened quietly and promised to put the record straight. I was never annoyed or insulted by that signals officer again. How he ever got to be an officer, I'll never know. I had carried my burden far too long; it was becoming too heavy. I realised it would take many more years to be free of the aftershocks of extreme mental stress and battle fatigue. One must live such an experience to fully understand the complaint.

### *Tada-U and Mandalay — 1945:*

About this time the Japs were roving around in large groups heading south avoiding contact as far as possible. They were ridden with disease, short of food and no longer the arrogant 'invincible' champions over the western world. They raped and plundered wherever they set foot, using their captives as slaves or concubines. They abandoned the very old and very young in burned-out villages, without grain or animals to sustain the poor innocent victims' survival, where they died of starvation, and that is how we found them.

A British armoured unit broke loose from the main advance and headed south towards Meiktila where they massacred a large number of enemy personnel who were caught completely by surprise. A group of Royal Scots set up a few highly successful ambushes which did more than level the score. We swung left for the railway yards at Tada-U (Amarapura).

En-route I had the occasion to take cover by jumping into a dried-up nullah, but my foot landed badly on a rock causing a bad sprain. However, I got up, eventually marching the last ten miles to Tada-U in extreme agony, hoping it would soon come right.

The Camerons were sweeping to the left of us and reached the railway first. It was soon evident that it was operational and they tapped the telephone line while a Burmese official was speaking to someone at the other end. An interpreter was brought forward and soon it was discovered that a troop train was due, travelling south from the direction of Mandalay. The artillery sent over a ranging shot, which startled the voice on the telephone (he was the stationmaster). By listening to his excited comments, the RA were able to correct the instructions to their gunners and found their target by remote control. The train was duly shot up on arrival at the station causing more confusion among the Jap HQ personnel already on the run from Fort Dufferin (Mandalay).

We arrived at Tada-U to find a captured railway engine with steam up, hissing up and down the line manned by a few grinning squaddies who had just recently taken over the new ownership. The line ran south towards Kyaukse as Tada-U was the end of the line north, since the demolition of the rail bridge, whose steel rails and girders were wide apart and gaping skywards — a sight to remember.

A determined pocket of Japs were shooting it out across the road from us and seemed determined to commit hari-kari as they could only surrender otherwise. We had the whole area surrounded. An air strike was called and after every dive-bombing attack there was a pause, after which they would start shooting again and again. Finally they were left under surveillance, as the sappers had now finished the pontoon bridge across the wide stream ahead while under constant fire from the enemy groups trying to filter through our lines.

We crossed under an umbrella of covering fire from a section of Mk 8 Vickers machine-guns manned by the Manchester or Middlesex Regiment. The Camerons were our next of kin, so we didn't mind them getting to Mandalay first (from the south), as the main attack had been made by other units from the north.

## Mandalay at Last — 1945:

We settled in just north of Tada-U occupying a rice paddy field. My foot was no better so I saw the MO who took one look and simply said, "You have broken two small bones on the bridge of your foot." I could not believe it at first, but the doc wrapped my foot with a broad Elastoplast strap, and the support helped to ease the aching pain.

The battalion received a beer ration, the first since Christmas, and it was a great treat after drinking nothing but chlorinated water all those long weary months. We were allowed to take off our boots that night. What a great relief that was, as our feet seldom saw the light of day and socks could have been removed more easily with a jackknife! Shortly after settling down for the night, there was a commotion between the rows of sleeping men slightly inebriated by the beer ration. A soldier had called out to someone lurking past in the grey dark of a moonless night, asking him for a light, but got no response. This caused him to take notice and promptly threw a boot at the silent intruder. He was clean bowled first shot — not a maiden, but he turned out to be a Jap! The whole platoon crowded round the luckless victim and escorted him to HQ for interrogation. It was later discovered that the prisoner was well educated, spoke perfect English and was carrying maps and other information valuable to our side. He did not believe in hari-kari and was prepared to do a deal whereby he left for Division HQ shortly afterwards. The war was over for him.

Mandalay had fallen. We were due a well-earned rest and there was an air of relaxed relief. The camp was a rest area and our colonel arranged for us to go by truck in small groups and see this mystic city of the Orient. I went with one of the first liberty trucks and the carnage of war was evident along either side of the road. The Camerons had given the Japs a fitting farewell. No more would we have those poor souls to bother us. The city was derelict and there were very few buildings left standing. The brewery was unoperational, much to the disappointment of the army personnel. The Japs had left us nothing worth having. The pagoda at the top end of the town was intact and we visited the shrine of the Reclining Buddha.

From there we went to Fort Dufferin, which was the last enemy stronghold before they slipped out the back door after being under siege from the troops attacking from the north. The walls were twenty-four feet thick and they withstood the onslaught of aerial bombardment as well as the point blank shelling by 5.5 field guns. When we visited the fort there were cartons of brown boots left behind by the previous occupants and on inspection, it was found that they were too wee for the average soldier, but one or two pairs were taken by those who could wear them. Much later those who took the boots discovered that they were made of cardboard, and tanned brown. The soles fell off when wet and the quartermaster was furious when they had to go to him for a new pair! They had slung their old British boots away, which meant they had to pay for them.

## *Back to India — 1945:*

After the fall of Mandalay, the Royal Scots were recalled to India to regroup and prepare for a naval assault on Rangoon. We moved across country to the junction of the Chindwin and Irrawaddy rivers, where we would board Dakotas running a shuttle service over the Lushai Hills to Nazir Hat, just east of Chittagong.

During this respite, as a tired and weary veteran I had time to reflect on the recent campaign now slipping behind us. I held nothing but admiration for those unsung heroes who would never be mentioned in any official history book. Apart from the ordinary soldier in the field, I also admired the lone carrier driver who operated the Wasp flame-thrower, and the RE bulldozer driver who rumbled back and forth all day and well through the night, clearing scrub while the shooting was still in progress, making forward airstrips to back up the front-line troops. The air force pilots and ground crews were also worthy of a mention. Without them our task would have been much more difficult. At long last, we had good organisation all the way down the line — a pleasant change from the 1942-43 Arakan Campaign.

The travelling time by road to Mandalay would have been around three weeks, while by air it only took two hours over the mountains! We slept by the runway overnight and shortly after dawn were lined up in groups of twenty — the payload for Dakotas. Gradually, as the planes landed, each group moved forward until finally our contingent climbed aboard. We had a Canadian crew who went by the book. They were well disciplined, and their quiet bearing reassured us and gave us confidence in them. We didn't want anything to go wrong now! Ten men sat on either side and our equipment was neatly roped down the middle. No smoking was allowed. The fuselage door was locked, then we taxied to the end of the dirt runway. I heaved a massive sigh of relief as we finally became airborne.

It was a clear day as we looked down on the jungle-clad hills below, steep and rugged. Somewhere down there lay the bodies of an air crew, alongside that legendary Chindit Commander Orde Wingate. There were conflicting stories about this unorthodox military genius. I never served under him, and therefore I cannot comment on the matter, but personally I was glad I didn't have to go with them on their missions impossible.

The runway at Nazir Hat was sealed for all-weather operations and I noticed that a linked, perforated steel decking was laid on the 'muttee' paddy and covered with heavily pitched rolls of felt sheeting. The sun did the rest by fusing the whole structure together very effectively. The war did induce some good ideas for the future of mankind!

The battalion finally travelled round the bay to Barrackpore, a few miles north of Calcutta and near Dum-Dum air base, occupying a first class tented camp formerly used by Americans, I think. It was a bit too good for the poor British soldier who was never pampered like our rich allies! We envied them, of course. They had better food, better clothes, better living quarters, treble the pay, the PX stores plus a restricted tour of duty abroad.

*25-pounder Howitzer*

## Rest and Peace — 1945:

It was now July 1945. The war was not yet over for any of us out east, although peace had come to Europe at long last. I signed on in April 1939 as a Terrier for four years and was now in my seventh year as an extended duty soldier for the duration of hostilities. A lot of us were 'brassed off' with our misfortune and looked forward to the day when we could take a well-earned rest, preferably in civvie street.

The army must have recognised our poor physical condition as the camp at Barrackpore was turned into a convalescent centre. We were fed chicken as a daily diet and fresh food of all kinds available, including a wide selection of fresh fruit, and told to eat as much as we liked. Seconds were always on the menu. There were proper showers, which added unheard-of luxury to our new lifestyle and we slept in American Army ridge tents with monsoon storm sheets over them, which provided a shaded air space above the tent proper. Our tent was under a tree laden with mangoes, which kept falling at regular intervals all around us as they became overripe. The chicos asked me if they could have some and I told them yes, provided they cleaned up the lot every day, as the sweet rotting fruit attracted all the insects over a ten-mile radius! They kept their part of the bargain and peace reigned over the camp.

I reported to the MO about my foot. He removed the broad Elastoplast strap and declared me fit. Yes, I could play soccer too, he assured me! So off I went and joined a team on the football field. The ball came straight to me and I instinctively met it with a swinging right foot and belted it up the centre. I fell in a heap, writhing in pain. The boys helped me back to the MO who simply said, "You've done it again!" So back to the plaster once more.

When going on leave I was paid 600 rupees (nine months' back pay), and along with two mates we decided on Darjeeling right up on the Himalayas where it was cooler. The weather was dull and overcast with mist and rain, but we soon settled down and went out pony riding every day among the surrounding foothills. When shopping in the bazaar we paid for tea to be sent home in small wooden chests at one of the many merchants shops. At the racetrack we lost a fortune on nags that stopped short of the post, while an upgraded outsider trotted in as winner. The races were all rigged and the bookies fixed the jockeys before the race! It was a good laugh just the same. They only did it once to us!

One day in the bazaar I was invited with a mate into a respectable shop and asked to take tea with the elderly owner. We chatted for a while, then he asked me if I was married or betrothed. I said "no", but was rather puzzled when he added, "Would you sahib, please marry my daughter?"

I thought it was meant to be a joke, but the old man was genuinely serious. Firstly she lived in Bombay, and Dad was only up in Darjeeling for the summer season. It was to be a business arrangement and I would be well rewarded. The contract would be for a minimum of two years, then I could decide whether to stay in India and manage his business warehouse in Bombay, or go back to Scotland alone. All he wanted was a pale-skinned offspring as a grandson! Believe it if you like, but I solemnly refused in spite of the wealth that was to be part of the deal. My mate offered to take my place, but the old man simply said, "It was not you that I asked, sahib!" He valued my very fair skin and red auburn wavy hair. I left the shop feeling intrigued but flattered. I was later intercepted by the old man's servant on one or two occasions when in town, but I refused to go back and reconsider. I avoided that part of the bazaar as much as possible. I longed for Bonnie Scotland, and the surrounding hills made me all the more homesick.

On returning from Darjeeling, the battalion was getting ready to move. We duly entrained for an unknown destination, moving off in a southerly direction. The journey seemed endless, the terrain undulating. During an unscheduled night stop we could hear muffled voices near the side of the track. Some of the lads said they were a colony of baboons but we didn't venture out to investigate — they could be vicious in a mob.

Somewhere along the line, news came through that Rangoon had been evacuated without a fight and prisoners were abandoned to their own resources, whereby they finally laid a ground message to our own reconnaissance planes. Could Bob Picken be among them? I honestly thought it was possible. Time would tell.

The train stopped on the following night at a British-style railway station where we were greeted by turbaned bearers wearing coloured sashes. "Feesh and cheeps, sahib!" was the cry all along the troop train. The state ruler wished to honour us with his hospitality! We accepted his kind gesture and heartily partook of the elaborately prepared delicacy. I think we were just entering the state of Hyderabad, hence the celebration. It was nice to know that the British were still welcome in India.

The battalion finally arrived at Secunderabad, the new city of Hyderabad. I soon found on arrival that my old artillery battery was down the road a bit and I duly walked in one day and had a meal and a chat with some of the older rankers, now depleted in number. Many new faces could be seen scattered around the mess hall. We had a lot to talk about before I finally retraced my steps to our own lines.

One day I was called to Battalion HQ office and I confirmed my departure date from Britain: 5th January, 1942. The clerk told me I was being put up for repatriation as I had been out longer than the battalion. Ultimately, twelve of us were told to stand-by to move. It was great news and we started to count the minutes prior to our final departure for Deolali transit camp — my first camp in India! Many memories flashed through my mind, tortured by the horrors of war, sickness and death, and the personal loss of many friends. I had come out of it pretty lucky, as many never made it. The epitaph at Kohima reminded us of that: 'For their tomorrow, we gave our today'. I still remember.

### Homeward Bound — 1945:

The twelve-man repatriation squad duly arrived at Deolali about the end of July. There were some changes in the camp after three and a half years' absence, most obvious was a new dining hall, brick built with plastered walls inside. The whole camp had a new look about it, yet basically it was still the same I suppose. We saw our first Italian prisoners there. They had a free run of the compound and several of them were voluntarily engaged in painting Don Quixote murals on the new mess hall walls, much to the admiration of their British captors.

The seemingly long delay waiting for our draft to embark for home was understandable as shipping was arriving and leaving at very irregular intervals. While waiting, we retraced our steps down to the bazaar but found that the old bargaining repartee had gone as our American cousins simply paid whatever was asked and the poor British Tommy could not compete. There ended an era in British military history!

Early in August Hiroshima was atom bombed! There was stunned silence. Would Japan surrender? Then a few days later Nagasaki was also bombed. Japan got the message: unconditional surrender. The war was over after six long years. A letter arrived postmarked Delhi addressed to me and from none other than Bob Picken! My world was spinning back on its axis; it was good to be alive after all. The fog was clearing from my troubled mind. I could see hope for us all in the distant future.

Soon we were entrained for Madras and homeward bound at long last. As the long train pulled up alongside the wharf, the great ship towered above us. She was the *Stirling Castle* and had been diverted to Madras as they had a cable fouling one of her propellers. She was en route from Australia part laden with the wives and children of British troops who had been left behind at Hong Kong and Singapore, way back in 1941. Many would never see their loved ones again. We systematically filed towards the main gangway, watched by the scores of smiling faces of those already on board. As I took my turn up those memorable planks, I was met at the top by an old adversary with the rank of sergeant-major. He advanced towards me with outstretched hand saying, "Scotty, am I glad to see you! Shake hands and let bygones to bygones?" His eyes stared into mine, pleadingly.

I relented and replied in a gruff voice, "Perhaps it's for the best, sir. No more hard feelings."

We shook hands and went our separate ways in life. I could forgive my fellow man, a quality I cherished with inward pride, yet still remained humble.

The ship had been fitted out as a trooper over in the States and the tubular folding bunks were a great improvement on the old hammocks, which I detested. We were soon rounding Ceylon and heading across the Indian Ocean for Suez. All the blackout screens were removed and the trip became a relaxed and light-hearted affair. Everyone was willing to talk to one another as we all belonged to a newborn fraternity.

As I sat on deck watching some whales snorting air from the depths, a lad sat down beside me, obviously looking for a bit of company and I seemed to attract his troubled thoughts. He bluntly asked how old I thought he was. I pondered over his question as he was very serious, then I calmly stated he didn't look a day older than thirty-six! The man was balding with grey hair turning white and could have passed for being much older. He gave me a wan look, then simply said, "I am twenty-six!" Pulling out a wallet, he showed me a photograph of a young mother with a babe in her arms.

"Never mind" I said, "she'll be waiting for you when we get to Blighty."

There was a long silence. His eyes welled up and finally he told me they were both killed along with his parents during an air raid in London. He was an orphan.

I was stunned. As he had no other relative to turn to, what a homecoming! The WVS took care of the few like him on arrival at Liverpool. Meanwhile I kept an eye on him throughout the voyage as he was in a very disturbed state of mind.

I recalled the raids on London during the Battle of Britain. I had been down river and saw the Germans flying over in formations of 100, destined for the capital. Fighters were locked in combat above our heads and showers of spent cartridges came singing down like rain on top of us. We were helpless to do anything, and the people of London copped the lot. They were the true heroes of the war; we were only part-timers by comparison.

The ship stopped long enough to refuel at Port Said, but no one was allowed off. During that time, the *Strathmore* slipped past us, heading east, laden with white-kneed troops rigged out in Bombay bloomers. "Go and get your knees brown!" was the cry from our ship, while others yelled, "You're too bloody late!" — All in good fun, of course.

We looked towards de Lesseps' statue as the ship headed west once more, into the Mediterranean. The sea was like glass and beautiful hues of all shades were emanating from the deep blue water. It was good to be alive.

The Bay of Biscay was also calm and the turbulent currents could be seen branching like rivers across the ocean. We could feel the drift as the ship steered against the forces of nature. Grey skies loomed ahead. Orders were signalled: 'Proceed to Liverpool'. Sometime later a voice on the Tannoy drew our attention to a murky smudge on the horizon: "We are now off the coast of Wales!" There was one mighty cheer from the troops, and soon there was a trail of KD astern as the boys abandoned their tattered and torn tropical apparel, having changed over to warmer battledress issued at Deolali while waiting for a ship.

There was a prolonged delay at the Mersey Roadsted as our arrival was unexpected. We were to have gone into Southampton. However, the *Stirling Castle* eventually negotiated the well-defined marker buoys and tied up at Princes Pier. The wharf was fenced off and deserted. Then a lone young mother walked through the barrier, leading a wee toddler. She was a brave woman! A rousing chorus came from the troops lined against the rails. How she hoped to identify her long-lost husband was beyond most of us, but I believe he was eventually produced from the mass of faces lining the various decks. A solemn military band hurriedly appeared with the official welcome-home party. A few bars were played then an attempt was made to deliver a speech, but the VIP's words were drowned by irate heckling when we learned that we could not leave the ship until trains and other transport were made available. Delays in moments like these created a near mutiny, but gradually common sense prevailed and we managed to send off telegrams prior to disembarking next morning.

The train journey to Princes Street Station, Edinburgh was like a glide through fairyland. The coaches were so comfortable and the clickerty-click of wheels on the track seemed muffled. Everywhere we looked there were green fields, green hills, green trees, and no dust clouds! Our small 'draft' reported to Redford Barracks where we collected one month's pay and a repatriation leave pass. It was late in the day so we left for home the next morning.

One morning when I awoke, there was my mother, never a sentimentalist, standing by the bedroom door, a tear trickling down her cheek. "Son," she said, "what have they done to you?" I was only then aware of that ghoulish, haunted and starved look, revealed by sunken bloodshot eyes and hollowed cheeks. "I will have to feed you up again," she concluded as she turned away.

I was the youngest of three boys and she always looked on me as the baby. Mothers think we should never grow up! I could only eat a third of the food put down for me and it was decided that my stomach had shrunk as the food out east got scarcer.

I returned to the barracks at Edinburgh, and shortly after was posted to go on a draft to Germany! The notice was an insult to my idea of fair play. Here I was after six and half years' service, overdue for demob, yet because I was still classified as too young, had to serve another six months until demobbed under Group Twenty-eight — so they decided to send me off to Europe.

I was suffering from the severe cold; it was now November and I had not had time to acclimatise. I was still experiencing symptoms of malarial relapses, malnutrition, mental instability through shell-shock and the lingering effects of battle fatigue. I was further shocked and utterly demoralised. There were 3,000 troops continually passing through that holding barracks and the majority were unblooded youths eager to go overseas now that the war was over. It did not make sense.

I told the CSM that I was unfit and he put me on a special sick parade. He was going to show me a thing or two! That afternoon I was marched down the MI room and examined by a young medic just out of school. He passed me 'A1 all duties' on the CSM's instructions, and then marched out the door. "Right," I said, "that was a farce and I demand a full medical board!"

The CSM sneered, "You'll get one all right and a court martial!"

I simply replied "Suits me fine, sir."

Next day, with the young MO's approval, I was duly sent under escort up to Edinburgh Castle where I was marched at the double, cap off, into a room where I was confronted by a brigadier, a staff colonel, and a civilian doctor.

"Is this man on a charge, Corporal?"

"No, sir!"

"Then get out of here and stand outside. This matter is private!"

The veteran soldier kindly asked me to take a seat and state my case. I mentioned my foot injury at Tada-U, and asked him if he knew that part of the world? He replied with a resounding, "Yes, I was in Burma a long time ago, including Tada-U!" This was followed by the three heads getting together, an examination by the Canadian civilian, and I was unanimously declared unfit for further military duties. I was excused army boots, guard duties and all parades and allowed to wear civilian shoes!

The brigadier finalised by stating, "This man has done more than enough for his country already." Then privately he asked what my plans were as I could get demobbed on medical grounds, but I would forfeit all my long-service leave pay which amounted to, in my case around sixteen weeks' wages. I decided to stay until my group came up as I had no money. I returned to Redford Barracks.

The CSM was quite a character and short with bow legs. He had served nineteen years in the British Army, and was abroad only once when he went to Dublin to bring back a prisoner! He told me that he had no wish to return to civvy street as he had no trade to go back to. He used to sell newspapers on Princes Street and there was no future in that! The man had no specialist qualifications in the army and how he ever became a company sergeant-major no one could ever tell me. However he knew how to yell at and abuse people, so I suppose in the eyes of the army hierarchy he made a good warrant officer!

I handed the medical report to the CSM, who had a big smile on his face. I was due to leave within a day or so on that draft. As he stood and read it his face turned purple — "Jesus Christ, are you allowed to breathe?" The report was then handed to the company commander who quietly asked what I should do during the remainder of my stay at Redford. I volunteered to be a permanent barrack room orderly. The CSM agreed it was a good idea and we were quite good friends after that. He left me alone and I kept out of his way.

I took courses on rehabilitation studies to pass the time away, choosing economics, transport organisation and music; the latter strictly as an observer only, as I always appreciated good music though I could never play a note. The months dragged on until finally, with Group Twenty-eight, I was demobbed at York on the 2nd May, 1946. The Indian MO said he could only sign my discharge papers if I agreed to go out as A1, otherwise I would be referred to a military hospital for treatment, thereby delaying my discharge for at least another three months!

I left the British Army in disgust after more than seven years as a British-style Legionnaire, with five ribbons, a civvy suit, £81 sterling in my wallet plus a post office book which allowed me to draw sixteen weeks' army pay in fortnightly instalments. I was almost a free man. It had been more akin to a prison sentence and I was put on parole as a Z Reservist in perpetuity unpaid, along with five million other ex-civilians in uniform! I had a right to ask, "Who won the war anyway?"

Shortly after settling down at home, I received an OHMS letter saying that I owed the army £56 19s 6d as I had overdrawn my wages prior to my demob and it would be deducted from my leave allowance!

My mother said, "You are not in debt, are you son?"

I said "No, definitely not!"

She replied, "Then fight them!"

I grinned at her: she was a fighter too. She fought poverty when my late father was dying of tuberculosis over a period of fifteen years, with three sons to rear. I was proud of her fighting spirit. She needed the money and I was going to make sure that she got it! Our family supplied three boys to the army. My mother was a very lonely widow during those long war years — I owed her a lot.

I wrote to Infantry Records at Perth (Scotland), stating it would be necessary to send me a full statement of accounts as I was taking the matter up with the War Office through my MP and my lawyer, as I had proof that I was not in debt, having never overdrawn money in my whole career in the British Army. Within five days I received a registered reply, apologising for their error and asking me to accept a cheque for £16 16s as my number had been mistaken for someone else's. It was a beautiful cover-up. I pursued the matter no further, but I was not in credit either, to my knowledge!

I was a sleeper on Z Reserve until 1956 (yes, ten years) when I again received calling-up papers. This time it was for the Suez Crisis. The government was wanting to knock hell out of the Egyptians for nationalising the canal. It was purely political and I wanted no part in it; besides, who wanted an old crock like me anyway? Had they not had enough of me? After treating me like an insignificant nobody, I was classified as a specialist and it would appear that I was indispensable! What a hope! I sent the papers back, stating that I was medically unfit and would go to jail first anyway, adding that the army must be hard up for men! I never heard from them ever again, but I am still a Z Reservist after thirty-odd years, as far as I know. No one ever notified me otherwise.

I can still laugh at the whole affair, and owe Whitehall nothing. I was proud to have served my country and been a member of two great regiments: the Royal Artillery and the Royal Scots. My seven years' service was a great sacrifice on my part as the period encompassed my entire transition from youth to maturity. I was not ready for the outside world in civilian life; it took a lifetime to adjust. After all, what does one do with a vacuum?

WE SHALL, REMEMBER THEM ... *UBIQUE* (EVERYWHERE)

*The author*

*F Troop, O-P Carrier Crew, Deolali, India, March 1942.*
*Captain C. M. Butterworth (seated) seventh from left.*
*Bombardier Russell (bottom row) fourth from left.*
*Signaller Picken (second top row) seventh from left.*
*Driver/Signaller Bryden (second top row) eighth from left.*

*The author — 1943-44, Calcutta.*

# INSTRUCTIONS ON OPERATION
## OF SURRENDER PASSES

On the Divisional front we shall be air-dropping leaflets urging JAPANESE soldiers to surrender.

We know these leaflets will work if properly used. Similar leaflets caused JAPANESE to surrender at IMPHAL, KAMAING and MYITKYINA. These JAPANESE did not have to be blasted from fox holes. It cost no Allied lives to take them prisoner.

The percentage of JAP soldiers who attempt to surrender is not large but those who do will always talk. The prisoners whom we captured in our initial advance in the Railway Corridor gave us important information, which quite certainly helped us considerably in later stages of the attack. So everyone is invaluable. Our interrogation of him may save our lives later.

The leaflets serve as surrender tickets for the JAPS. A sample leaflet is attached. The English translation is on the back of this sheet. Examine it carefully. The conditions of surrender must be observed carefully by the enemy and by us. You will notice that the conditions are simple and general. But anyone who follows them will unmistakably be trying to surrender.

If the JAP does not observe the surrender conditions satisfactorily - shoot him. If he behaves correctly, however, hold your fire and prepare to take him prisoner. Surrender leaflets will quickly lose their value if a JAPANESE is shot by us while trying to surrender in good faith.

For your own protection be alert - take no chances. Don't go after any surrendering JAP - make him come to you. In this way the risks of ambush and deception can be avoided. An intelligently handled surrender does more than remove a potential killer from the ranks of the enemy - it almost always pays a dividend in information about the enemy's plans and dispositions.

*F. W. Festing*

Major General,
Commander,
36 Division.

# Translation of Japanese Surrender Pass

## INSIDE

OFFICERS & MEN OF THE JAPANESE ARMY!

Your bravery has won my praise - I am filled with pity for the tragic plight into which you have fallen.

As you already know the outcome of the battle has been constantly one-sided. As on Attu, the Marshalls and Saipan - and as in North Burma the final result has been annihilation of your forces.

Now, without hope of supplies or reinforcements, you are about to repeat this tragedy. With the outcome already clear, needless wounding and slaughtering of innocent soldiers is contrary to the aim of the Allied forces.

Then the havoc of war ends and the rebuilding of your nation begins, upon whom will your Fatherland depend to carry out this task? Your duty lies - not in sacrificing yourself in this useless battle, intoxicated in the name of "glorious death" but in guarding your life so that when the day of post-war reconstruction comes you can give your effort. This is the path of true patriotism and loyalty to the Emperor.

Although reported to have met glorious death, a number of your comrades are behind our lines living days of hope, receiving kind treatment, and possessing full guarantee of future security.

The present war began as a result of the ambitions of world conquest of the German dictatorship and the Japanese militarists. For the sake of world peace the Allied armies aim at the destruction of these tyrants. But they harbor no designs whatever against the welfare and happiness of the Japanese people.

You have fully done your duty as subjects and preserved your honor as warriors. I sincerely hope you will rely on the chivalry of our forces and instead of dying vainly - surrender to become brave warriors in rebuilding the New Japan.

This is my strong advice.

Commander of the Allied Forces

## INSTRUCTIONS

This paper is a safety pass.

1) Approach the Allied positions in daytime and carry no weapons.

2) Use the most suitable means to show clearly your possession of this pass.

3) If you do not have a pass, take appropriate steps to show that you have no hostile intentions.

4) If an Allied soldier signals you show him this pass. Follow his orders which will be given by signs.

## OUTSIDE

(In English & Chinese)

ALLIED TROOPS! The bearer of this pass is surrendering. He probably does not understand English, but has been instructed to follow your signs. Treat him courteously and conduct him to headquarters.

By order of:
The Commanding Officer

本證持有人係向我方投誠者雖或不諳華語惟本部

中國部隊注意

己看其服從手勢行動應即予優待並護送來部

指揮部令

**ALLIED TROOPS** The bearer of this pass is surrendering. He probably does not understand English but has been instructed to follow your sign. Treat him courteously and conduct him to headquarters. By order of: The Commanding Officer

SURRENDER

日本軍將兵諸子ニ告グ

諸子ノ勇猛果敢ナル防戰ハ敵ナガラモ讚嘆措ク能ハサル處ナリ

惜クモ諸子ハ既ニ絶望ナル戰局ニ在リ諸子ノ慘烈ナル奮鬪モ其ノ甲斐ナク戰局ハ再ビ反ヘス可カラサル所以ナリ

諸子モ識ルガ如ク我カ聯合軍ト日本軍トノ戰ハ如今全滅ノ悲運ニ終レリ今ヤ諸子ハ戰局ノ全般ニ於テ全ク孤立セントシ其ノ惨憺タル境遇ニ陷リタルハ寧ロ同情ニ堪ヘサルモノナリ

諸子ハ常ニ一方ニハ「アッツ島」「マーシヤル島」或ハ「サイパン」其他ノ諸島ニ於ケル如ク悲惨ナル最後ヲ遂ゲンコトヲ欲スルモ遂ニ得サルニ至レリ

諸子ハ滅ニ瀕ス增援補給ノ望ナク是等ノ絶望的態度ヲ以テ從來諸子ハ無益ナル多クノ犠牲ヲ忍ビ死ヲ賭シテ戰ヘリ諸子ノ祖國ハ何人ヲ俟チテカ身命ヲ投ゲ

諸子ノ輸收スルナク諸子ノ愛國ハ將來ニ世界平和ノ意義ヲ本トシ一切ニ建設的方面ニ向ハシメンコトヲ聯合軍ハ證シテ寧ロ諸子ノ爲メニ之ヲ樂クスルモノニ於テ椎ヒ聯合軍ハ寧ロ諸子ガ

國家ヲ爲メニ大義ニ死スルハ非ザルヲ慨ク現下ニ無益ニ殘虐スルコトナク敢然トシテ我カ後ヲ發

國ヲ愛シ君ヲ愛ス聯合軍ハ伊獨ノ總敗降後再建日本ニ對シテ諸子ノ祖國ニ王將建ノ日ヲ待ニ希望ヲ確メラル

大義ニ於テ保テ日本軍將ノ切ノ世界役目ノ野望ヲ以テ我カ聯合軍ハ敗兵ヲ屠ルニアラス諸子ノ將ヲ戰ヲ以テ途ニ王將ニ待殺ノ世ト從ヘリ獨リ伊獨鐵等ノ殘虐ニ從撃シ諸子ノ役目的トシ日本國民ノ安

聯合軍ハ民土ノ近道ニ信ジ武官ノ陶醉セル膽コトナクシテ我方ニ投ジ我方ニ確認スル希クハ

諸子ガ新日本建設ニ武士ノ勇士タレ陶醉ノ賣ルコトナク

右ハ新日本建設ニ勸告ス

　　　　　　　　　　　　　　聯合軍司令官

———◆———

本紙ヲ安全通過證トス

一、書面ハ聯合軍陣地ニ近ヅクトキ導ク但シ兵器ハ絶對ニ持タヌ事若シ本通過證ヲ所持セサル場合ハ臨機ノ處置ヲ以テ聯合軍兵士ニ絶對無抵抗ノ意志ヲ表示シ本證ヲ示シ聯

二、合軍兵士ノ命令ニ從フ事

三、適宜ノ方法ヲ以テ本通過證ヲ所持スル所ヲ表示スル事

右ハ我ガ兵士ノ手段ニ依リ聯合軍ヨリ命令ニ從フ事

本通過證ハ表面ノ英語及ビ支那語ヲ日本語譯文ヲ以テ示ス

　　　　　　　　　　　　　　聯　合　軍　司　令　官

10 Castelnau
Barnes
London  SW13 9RU

30th June 1995

Mr  W M Bryden
35 Curror Street
Selkirk
Scotland  TD7 4HG.

Dear Mr Bryden

Many thanks for your letter. I'm relieved to know that the Appreciation is OK after all.

Good news  −  the tape has turned up. Here it is, with a backup copy for good measure. I've kept one for myself  −  I hope you don't mind.

I was gripped by your account of those first weeks in the Arakan. Your description of people and events is masterly. I remember all the equipment so well (including the helio) that the scenes come to life for me very easily.

As an old-time Gunner, I understand the full horror of what happened on Conical Hill  −  the human carnage at the OP, the nightmare journey back and the silence when you arrived at the gun position, with no-one wanting to face the reality of it. I can grieve with you.

Best wishes for the future.

Yours

Arthur Sisson

(BRIG.)   A A SISSON
RETIRED

Dear Sir,

Colonel Kenyon's knee-jerk reaction to my letter supporting Martin McLane's experience at Donbaik was not entirely unexpected, but he quite innocently highlighted the problem when he referred to WW1 and the North West Frontier strategy; and appaling casualties, and the loss of so many young subalterns: The same strategy was applied by our top-brass in Delhi during 1942-43 when they ordered that "Donbaik was to be taken with the bayonet as in WW1" That order was first conveyed to the Inniskillings in early January 1943 as the planned advance on Akyab was blocked at Donbaik. The attack on the 6th Jan 1943 (Ref: Slim's Defeat into Victory) was an utter failure which involved about four Valentine tanks and the odd bren carrier, on highly unsuitable terrain. It was then decided to bring up the elite 6th Inf Bde plus the 1st Royal Scots, with air-support from a few dive-bombers. The casualty list was horrific but the result was the same as portrayed by Martin McLane.

The end came when 6-I-B HQ at Indin was overrun by Japanese "Imperial Guards". The 494 Battery, RA with 8 gun 25 pounders was cut off at the rear until we made for the beach adjacent to Bde HQ where we fired over open sights into the Jap positions until all our ammo was expended including HE, AP and smoke. We then limbered up and headed North to safety. It was then that Brigadier Cavendish could have been killed.

_In Summary:_ The battle of Donbaik lasted almost three months and was doomed to failure. The futile attacks on the Jap bunkers could have been avoided but we had no Naval support of any kind, not even a rowing boat when forced to retreat along the beaches. The whole campaign was ill conceived from the beginning, we used the forthcoming monsoon as an excuse to withdraw back to Maungdaw where I was hospitalised to Calcutta on board the 'Wusueh' hospital ship with malaria and a nasty leg wound.

Much later on I joined the 1st Royal Scots at Kohima and marched with them all the way to Mandalay. Fortunately I survived but never forgot my shell-shock ordeal as a signaller down the Arakan, the date was 4 January 1943, my Battery Commander, Major WM Breckinridge, died beside me. He was a highly respected TA officer and a true gentlemen.

_Footnote:_ The first two years of my training as a 'gunner' was with WWI equipment including 4.5 Howitzers, 18 Pounders, and French 75mm guns. I used a WWI Heliograph at Donbaik; and our instructors were men who served in France, Gallipoli, Gaza and India. Perhaps Colonel Kenyon may find that interesting.

As for my personal outlook: I have no wish to be embroiled in any personal vendetta, I still feel sorry for the families who lost their loved ones especially those who fell at Donbaik/Arakan Campaign in 1943. Also I believe in the unwritten golden rule - "No names - No pack drill".

WM McCulloch Bryden
130 Regt. RA. T.A.     Selkirk

_LETTER To "DEKHO"._
_2001_

Mr W M Bryden
35 Curror Street
SELKIRK TD7 4HO

Maesawelon
Gwyddgrug
Dyfed SA39 9AX
0559-384-742

18th November 1994

Dear Bill

Your two envelopes were awaiting my return home last night.
Enclosed the original of your "First Arakan" which I have
photocopied. Your type is with my friend Jane being
typed. As soon as she has done that I will get
it copied and return the original to you.

Everything you write is solid gold – TRUTH.

Got back yesterday from two days with Guy Powell 494 Bty
who remember your histo. Also have had two        'F' Troop
telephone conversations with Archie Birkyrere and hope
(494 Bty)
to get his story on tape.

On my way back from York, where Guy lives, I
called to see John Butterworth. (WIDOW CAPT. COLIN BUTTERWORTH)
"F" TROOP COMMANDER

I told them about your output and both are impressed.
So can I keep it up

Yours very sincerely

Noel Laws (CAPT. 316th)

P.S. 316 Bty 130 Field forced me at 19 into a man
R.A.                              (AGE)

**House of Lords**

W Bryden Esq
28 Elm Park
Selkirk TD7 4DY

27th April 2004

Dear Mr. Bryden,

I was most touched to receive your excellent book about your time in India
and Burma. I have thoroughly enjoyed reading it and I think it is a
tremendous effort on your part and I congratulate you. It is also good to
read and you were in a fine Regiment. You should take this comment as a
great accolade from me as after leaving the Indian Army and Gurkhas I went
to my mother's brother's Regiment, The Argyll and Sutherland Highlanders,
so that is two good Regiments!

Sadly I cannot get up to the Burma Star reunion in Perth this year but I know
your President Sir Eric Yarrow will be there and our Chairman Captain
Paddy Vincent RN will also be there.

With my thanks and warmest wishes.

Yours sincerely

John Slim